John Little spent 25 years worki⸺ ⸺⸺⸺ ⸺⸺ucer in
television current affairs before b⸺ ⸺ull-time author. He
has written eight books, including *The Hospital by the River*
(with Dr Catherine Hamlin); *Down to the Sea*; *Jem, a Father's
Story; Christine's Ark* and *Catherine's Gift*. He lives with his wife,
Anna, and son, Tim, on Sydney's northern beaches.

jdlittle@bigpond.com

MAALIKA

My life among the Afar nomads of Africa

VALERIE BROWNING
and JOHN LITTLE

PAN
Pan Macmillan Australia

First published 2008 in Macmillan by Pan Macmillan Australia Pty Limited
This Pan edition published in 2009 by Pan Macmillan Australia Pty Limited
1 Market Street, Sydney

National Library of Australia
Cataloguing-in-publication data:

Browning, Valerie.
Maalika: my life among the Afar nomads of Africa/
Valerie Browning and John Little.

978 0 3304 2474 5 (pbk.)

Browning, Valerie.
Human rights workers—Biography.
Nurses—Biography.
Afar (African people)—Social life and customs.
Ethiopia—Description and travel.

Little, John, 1942-

323.092

Typeset in 13/15.5pt Granjon by Midland Typesetters, Australia
Printed in Australia by McPherson's Printing Group

Cartographic art by Laurie Whiddon

Papers used by Pan Macmillan Australia Pty Limited are natural, recyclable
products made from wood grown in sustainable forests. The manufacturing
processes conform to the environmental regulations of the country of origin.

To my children, Aisha and Rammidos

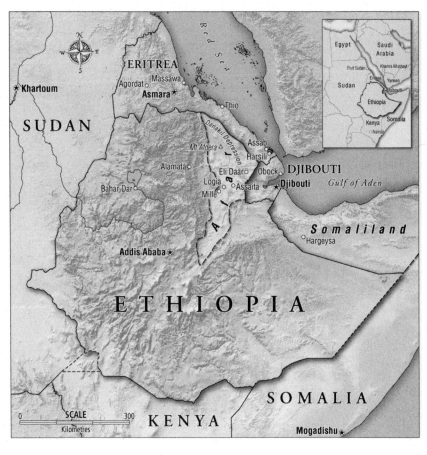

Ethiopia, showing the Afar region, bordered by Eritrea and Djibouti

To give and not count the cost.
To fight and not heed the wounds.
To toil and not seek rest.
To labour and not ask for any reward,
save that of knowing that we do your will.

St Ignatius of Loyola

FOREWORD by John Little

Some places are not meant to support life. The desert in the Horn of Africa is one. Summer temperatures reach 45 to 50 degrees Celsius. It's so hot that it hurts just to breathe. There's nowhere to escape the sun. The landscape is sand and rock, with the odd spiky plant stubbornly clinging to life. Scorpions, or maybe camels, might manage to survive here; it's hard to imagine that people would.

Yet some do.

They are called the Afar. They are nomads, wandering from waterhole to waterhole over an area encompassing Djibouti, at the entrance to the Red Sea, Eritrea and northern Ethiopia. They care nothing for borders, nor for laws other than their own. They disdain the planting of crops, and their only commerce is selling an occasional animal when they need cash. They own practically nothing. A family's entire possessions, house included, can be carried on the back of a camel.

Their appearance is striking. Some say the Afar are descended from the Pharaohs. They have ebony skin; the men typically have a broad forehead framed by a hairstyle right off the walls of an Egyptian tomb, which they artfully arrange into myriad corkscrew curls, dressed with butter. They wear a short sarong, sandals, their chest is bare and at the waist they carry a large curved knife.

Afar women are tall and slim with the fine features typical of the Horn. They are very often arrestingly beautiful. They wear long, brightly patterned dresses with sometimes a red-and-blue striped T-shirt, or occasionally nothing at all on top. Their long black hair is parted in the middle, sometimes plaited into numerous corn rows and held behind with a twist of cord. They enhance this outfit with necklaces or headbands made of brightly coloured plastic beads.

A family's wealth, if you could call it that, is in their animals – generally goats and camels, although in some less arid areas they may own cattle. The Afar diet consists mainly of bread and milk, so anaemia is common. They set up camp near a water source, graze their animals until the fodder runs out, then move on.

The water may be anything up to 10 kilometres distant. Fetching water is women's work. They have to walk to the source and back at least once a day carrying the load on their backs, and often a baby as well. Women also look after the children, milk the goats, make butter, grind the flour, and cook the hard little loaves of unleavened bread. The men look after camels or cattle, sell animals and buy goods for the family when they make a rare visit to a town.

The Afar live in low, dome-shaped huts made of woven palm matting spread over sticks. You enter by stooping double through a low opening. Inside there's a raised sleeping platform made of sticks sewn together with animal hide. There's no mattress. Opposite, a few stones make a fireplace where cooking is done. There's no chimney, the smoke simply seeps out through the matting, so when the fire is alight the atmosphere inside is pungent.

Nearby there will be a container made of woven palm fronds (smoked, so that they won't leak), used for milking, a butter container made of animal skin, a cooking pot and a tin box for bits and pieces.

They live without luxuries of any kind. No radio; no books, for they cannot read; nothing soft or frivolous; nothing that does not have a practical use. Their life is a hard, relentless struggle for survival. They are hostage to famine, locust plagues and, in some areas, other hostile tribes. If they get sick from cholera, typhus, diphtheria, malaria or any of a host of other ailments, there's no hope of reaching a hospital. One in three children dies before the age of five.

Who would choose to live in a place like this if they were not born to it?

Valerie Browning – Maalika – comes from Australia, one of the most privileged countries on earth. She is married to an Afar clan elder, Ismael Ali Gardo. They have two children: a girl, Aisha; and a boy, Rammidos. Valerie lives and works with the Afar – and she looks it. She's slightly built, with skin burnt dark brown by the desert sun. Her face is deeply lined, she has a couple of missing teeth and her long grey hair runs riot down to her shoulders. She hasn't worn lipstick or other makeup for decades. She owns half a dozen dresses, a headscarf or two, a wedding ring, a tattered Bible and that's about it.

She's tough. Stories abound of her marching in furnace-like heat for tens of kilometres while the men drop by the wayside with exhaustion. She has a firebrand temper and she doesn't brook nonsense from anyone – Muslim men included. She dresses like an Afar and speaks the language fluently. Really, she *is* Afar.

Just before this book was completed, she had been in Mabay in the centre of the Afar region in northern Ethiopia, carrying out a childhood vaccination program against diphtheria, tetanus, whooping cough, hepatitis B and influenza. It was summer, the time of year when the *harror*, or 'furnace wind', blows. It begins at noon and blasts across the desert until six at night. Think of a fan-forced oven. While the *harror* blows, the air is gritty with flying sand. If you open your mouth, the saliva cakes all the way down your throat.

This country destroys motor vehicles. To get to the vaccination area, Valerie and her helpers had to drive to the nearest town then walk for fourteen hours. The vaccines were carried on camels, in insulated containers filled with ice. Over a week, Valerie and the others walked for 300 kilometres seeking out isolated families.

At one stage, a young man of twenty, who they'd brought along to record the vaccinations, collapsed from exhaustion. His eyes were rolling and he was gabbling incoherently. They rehydrated him with a solution of salt and sugar in water, and kept on going. A day or two later Valerie's legs began to swell, due, she thinks, to an overload of the rehydration mix. She switched to a new water bottle and forced herself to continue. Right towards the end of the trip they were force-marching through a moonless night to pick up more ice when Valerie stepped into a hole and twisted her ankle. She fell to the ground and when she tried to get up, felt 'this fantastic pain'. She said to her health workers, 'Boys, my leg's gone.'

The ice pickup was still four hours away. Valerie's first thought was for the vaccines. She ordered the men to continue on with the camels and get more ice while she waited where she was.

When they returned, one of the men massaged her ankle, and applied some ice. She stood up, staggered, then, with the aid of a stick, started walking. 'I pushed myself and I found if I pushed myself, the pain went.'

When she's not out in the field, Valerie lives with her family in Logia, a baking, dust-blown town in northern Ethiopia. From there she runs the Afar Pastoral Development Association (APDA), which employs more than 500 people bringing health and literacy programs to the Afar.

My wife, Anna, and I went on two trips with her, me to observe and make notes, Anna to take photographs. They were short trips, nothing like that hellish trip into Mabay, but they gave us an insight into her hard, uncomfortable existence.

Small things illustrated her grit. She always insisted that we have the one passenger seat in the Toyota. She rode in the back, usually perched on a spare tyre, bouncing about violently as we lumbered over rough terrain, happily chatting away to the Afar workers accompanying us. At the end of one long day we stopped at Darsa Gita, a dusty little town of stick-and-mud huts on a main truck route. Valerie had organised a bed for us in the home of a schoolteacher. She and the others slept on the ground outside, within metres of the gravel road. All night long, trucks thundered noisily by. Each time one passed, the sleepers were enveloped in clouds of dust and exhaust fumes. In the morning, Valerie woke as cheerful and energetic as if she'd spent the night in a comfortable hotel.

After three days on the road, we arrived back in Logia in the middle of the afternoon. Tired, hot, caked with dust, we were craving clean clothes and a shower. Valerie went straight to the office and worked as usual until well after dark.

She is forceful, passionate, driven, quick to anger, sometimes abrupt, and completely selfless in her devotion to the Afar people. She can also be very funny. When we first arrived she'd just returned from the western part of the Afar regional state where she'd been fighting an outbreak of acute watery diarrhoea. The victims' poo looked like milk, she said. She'd never seen anything like it. APDA's drama team, which helps educate people about good health practices, had been with her. Describing the songs they'd made up, Valerie jumped to her feet and, with a big grin on her face, launched into an impromptu performance: 'Diarrhoea doesn't care if you are tall or short, it strikes everyone. Wash your hands with soap, da de da de da,' she trilled. Everyone broke up laughing.

One day we left her behind in a small town, meeting with some health workers, and travelled out into the desert to visit an Afar encampment. In the middle of nowhere we came across a group of nomads walking along. They were untouched desert people. The men had long, buttered hair and in addition to their knives they carried rifles, as there were raiders from another tribe about. The women were elegant, wearing bright dresses and traditional bead jewellery. Seeing the APDA logo on our vehicle, one of them came to the driver's window and asked, 'Where's Maalika?'

The driver told her. She enquired after Maalika's health and then she wanted to know about the children: 'How is Aisha? And Rammid?' She then asked after Ismael. Satisfied that all was well, she waved us on.

Maalika means 'Queen' in Arabic. And I suspect this was how that Afar woman regarded Valerie. She didn't know Maalika personally, but she was aware of what she was doing for her people, and for that, Valerie had the woman's loyalty. I'm certain Valerie would find this analogy too fanciful by far, for she is uncomfortable with praise. She says she's just doing a job that needs to be done. Forget about the airy-fairy stuff. But she also has the Christian belief in a calling – what Muslims think of as destiny. Whatever it is that drives her, it adds up to a remarkable life; one, I think, that needs to be acknowledged in the wider world.

Avalon Beach

CHAPTER 1

The time has come to tell my story. Not that I'm dying or anything, far from it. I am 56 years old, yet I still feel as strong as I did as a young woman. I can walk all day in the heat of summer, and I enjoy it. I'm looking forward to many years yet, living and growing with my husband, Ismael, my daughter, Aisha, my son, Rammid, and my beloved Afar people; many more years roaming the sparse wastes of northern Ethiopia, eating my favourite food, camel's milk and bread; blissful nights sleeping on the ground under the clear desert sky, far from the cares of a chaotic world. I know, of course, that the future can never be certain. Living far from so-called civilisation, I have learnt to be fatalistic. My Muslim brothers have a phrase they use often – *inshallah*, God willing. And although I am a Christian living in their world, it expresses my feelings exactly.

I do not seek fame. I am only telling my story now because soon it may be too late. My life is linked with the Afar people – Ismael's people – an ancient, nomadic race with a language of their own, and a mode of living I deeply respect. Their story is interwoven with my story, and the stark fact is that the Afar are facing cultural extinction. By telling you about my life, I hope to persuade the wider world to value the Afar as I do. If I fail, I fear they may go the way of the Australian Aborigines, the American Indians and that whole sad list of dispossessed people which shames the human race.

Friends in the developed world have told me that they could not live as I do. I have never understood why. Here in the harshest region of one of the poorest nations on the planet, I have everything I want: family, friendships, work that I love. What more do you need? Yes, it's a hard life, but to me it's one of those western lives which would be unendurable. I could not bear to live in some affluent country. I would find the abundance shocking.

My mother, who influenced me all her life, would say, 'That's all very well, Valerie, but you need to begin at the beginning, dear.' And so I shall, in a country and a culture as far removed from Ethiopia as you can find.

I spent the first ten years of my childhood on a dairy farm outside the village of Ripe in Sussex, England. I was the fifth of eight children. My mother was a tender and gracious lady who was adored by every one of her children. She never knew her own parents, as they had both died when she was three, in the influenza epidemic of 1919. She was brought up by a succession of aunts and uncles. Perhaps her own loss is what made her such a sweet and perfect mother. She never wanted wealth or possessions beyond what was necessary to live in modest comfort. This was just as well because Father was never any good at making money. My big brother David tells me that Father never paid income tax in his life because he never earned enough!

Our father was a hard, stubborn man. He was regarded by his children with respect bordering on fear. Some of us find it difficult to speak of him with much affection. In his youth he had studied at an agricultural college, graduating in the midst of the Depression. Unable to find employment, he travelled to Canada, where he worked on a wheat farm. From there, he went to what was then Rhodesia, to work on a tobacco farm.

In 1936, Mother – Barbara Barnes, as she was then – was in her final year of nursing, working in the Children's Hospital at Brighton. One day the matron arrived at her ward with two visitors, a Colonel Browning and his son, John. Mother already knew John slightly, as at one stage she had lived with her grandmother next door to his parents in Brighton. She remembered often hearing loud arguments which had culminated eventually in divorce.

At the hospital the two young people talked and were attracted to one another. Soon they began going out together. In 1938, when Mother was 21, they became engaged. Before getting married, Father wanted to try his hand at farming in Australia, so he went off to work on a wheat farm in Roma, Queensland. Mother was planning to follow him when he had settled in, but Adolf Hitler put a stop to that.

When it was obvious that war was about to break out, Colonel Browning ordered his son home. Mother and Father married in July 1939 and, almost immediately, Father was sent off with the British Expeditionary Force to fight in southern France.

While he was away, my brother David was born. In 1942, Father went with the Eighth Army, commanded by Field Marshal Lord Montgomery, to North Africa. Soon after the first Allied victory at El Alamein, Mother gave birth to another boy. It's typical of my father that he sent her a telegram from Tripoli instructing her what to call him: George after the king, and Victor for victory. There was no discussion; that was what he wanted, and Mother, as she would all her life, dutifully obeyed.

One of the many strange things about my father was that for three and a half years of the war he never came home. We found out afterwards that he could have obtained leave, but he just didn't bother. Why not is a mystery. George suspects things happened to him in the war which we don't know about. He probably had run-ins with his superiors, as he always had great difficulty with authority. George, like all of us, had an uneasy relationship with him. When George was twenty he went to theological college, planning to offer for the ministry. Father told him there were plenty of useless clergy in the church and he didn't need to add to their number. Father also tried to stop his marriage to his fiancée, Margaret. George went on to become a bishop and has been happily married to Margaret for 43 years. Ironically, at the age of 60, my father became an Anglican minister himself!

Mother lived in a flat in Brighton for the first part of the war. When the bombs started falling she stuck it out for a while, but when George got a piece of shrapnel through his pram she decided it was time to go somewhere safer. She went to a village on the edge of the South Downs. When the war ended and Father came home, they moved to the farm Grandfather had bought before the war. It was only 70 acres, mainly dairying with a herd of 30 cows, and a bit of cropping. Later, Father bought another 13 acres, bringing the total to 83, but it was still a constant struggle making enough money to live on.

There were eventually eight children in the family. Father could never remember the names of the younger ones. Introducing us, he would say, 'There's David, George, Rosemary, Nicholas and the four little ones.'

Father had been an army captain during the war, and he ran his family like a military unit. The evening meal was eaten promptly at five o'clock. In later years, when the four oldest children were going to grammar school in Lewes, their bus didn't drop them off until five fifteen. Still, the meal time never changed. I would already be at the table when they'd come in. Before they were allowed to sit down, they had to excuse themselves for being late.

There were never family discussions at the dinner table. Conversations consisted of Father voicing his opinions about things and the rest of us listening. You could never disagree with him. Once he had made his mind up about some subject, that was it. We were expected to pay attention in polite silence.

I remember we had a bread-slicing machine. At meal times the bread was issued according to a strict formula. It might be two slices for the oldest, one and a half for the next, one for younger ones and half a slice for the very youngest. The correct number of slices was cut before the meal and no variation would be tolerated.

My mother always supported Father, even though she may have had misgivings about the way he brought us up. Many women would have been discontented with her life. I'm sure she often had to suppress her own wishes in deference to him, but her loyalty never wavered. She was completely devoted to her husband and family, and I have no doubt that gave her all the fulfilment she wanted.

We produced our own vegetables and eggs. What we didn't eat ourselves, we sold. We often ate rabbit, which we had trapped ourselves. Although there were very few luxuries, we never went hungry.

The children all had chores to do. I started washing the dishes when I was five, standing on a chair to reach the sink. From a very early age, David and George were expected to help out around the farm. When he was eight, David was in charge of a great brute of a tractor which had to be cranked to start. It was terribly dangerous even for a grown man. While they were still schoolboys, he and George often had to lug 2¼ hundredweight sacks of wheat around (about 115 kilograms). George left school at fifteen to work on the farm full time. David had to get up early on Sunday mornings to help him do the milking.

At seven, my oldest sister, Rosemary, was expected to be Mother's helper. It was her responsibility to change nappies, help feed the little ones and to rock the babies to sleep. Father had no tolerance for babies. If we were eating a meal and a baby started grizzling, Rosemary would be ordered to go upstairs and 'stop that baby crying'.

My parents were both serious about their Christian faith, but they approached it very differently. Mother had a compassionate – I would say, Christ-like – understanding of faith. She always had great empathy with the underdog. Father's version of Christianity was more dogmatic. He interpreted the Bible literally. We learned about the wrath of God and the fires of hell. He drummed into us a strong sense of our responsibility to do something useful with our lives, as did Mother, only in a less doctrinaire way.

The requirement to serve influenced all of our lives. George is the Bishop of Canberra and has a deep interest in environmental matters. David has retired after a career as an obstetrician and gynaecologist. Nick worked in Central Australia on land rights with the Pitjantjatjara people. Rosemary and her husband, Ray, worked with the Church Missionary Society among Aboriginal people at Oenpelli in East Arnhem Land. Rosemary's now an Anglican minister on the Central Coast of New South Wales. Jackie and her husband, Brian, also worked with Aboriginal people in the Northern Territory. Brian is now a Baptist minister, and they live in country New South Wales. Pauline was a schoolteacher and still works part time. Carolyn is married to a farmer, Bob McCormack, in Junee, New South Wales. And me . . .? But I'm getting ahead of my story.

On Sundays we'd get up early and get ready to go to the village church. Rosemary had to polish ten pairs of shoes, George and David would be out at five a.m. milking, the other children would all be doing some chore or other. It must have been hard work for Mother getting us all ready. We'd pile into Father's little van, our parents in the front and the children rushing so that the first two in the back could claim the coveted spots on the mudguards. The rest had to sit on the floor. At church we'd take our place in the two front rows on the right-hand side – everyone knew that this was the Brownings' spot.

I don't want to create the impression that I was an unhappy child or deprived in any way. Quite the contrary. I have rosy memories of playing in the hedges around the farm, picking prim-roses and bluebells in the fields, sneaking up on the cows when they were lying down chewing their cud and jumping onto their backs. We used to ride our bikes 3 kilometres to the village school. In winter when it snowed, we'd put on layers of clothing topped off with a scarf which Mother would fasten at the back with a big safety pin so it wouldn't come off. We enjoyed life and had no idea that our upbringing was any more strict than was usual.

We had a third parent in my mother's sister, Auntie Joan. She always came to stay at Christmas and Easter, and sometimes took us to Brighton for the holidays. We'd visit the circus and the pantomime, paddle in the sea and generally have a wonderful time.

I'm told I was strong-willed and quite bossy as a little girl. My soul mate was my brother Nick, who is two and a half years older than me. He was a very naughty little boy, always getting into mischief. He wagged school a lot. I teamed up with him in quite a few of his escapades. I remember once at school catching a little girl so that Nick could try to drown her in the washroom. We both got into terrible trouble for that.

When I was ten years old Father announced to the family that we'd have to leave the farm as he simply could not make a living anymore. There were two choices: we would go to Scotland or Australia. Some of my siblings thought that Australia would be a great adventure, but to me it sounded awful. I begged Father to take us to Scotland. Mother preferred Scotland too but, as usual, Father made the final decision and that was that.

Before we left, I needed to have an operation for a congenital defect which had begun to give me trouble. It's called dysplasia. It's a malfunction of the osteoclasts, the cells which are responsible for moulding the long bones as they grow. The result is that exostoses, or knobs, grow at the end of the bones. They'd first discovered it when I was a baby. They found I had crooked fingers and thought at first that I'd broken them by sticking them through the metal sides of my pram. I was being cared for by a specialist in Eastbourne. He recommended that I have an operation on my fingers to correct the deformity before I went to Australia, as he thought doctors there wouldn't know about the disease.

The operation was done and I spent a couple of months in hospital recovering. Later, in Australia, when I was seventeen, I had a spike of bone removed from my inner upper right arm, as it had grown to the point where I had extreme pain whenever I tried to pick anything up. From then on I had no more surgery. I was advised by an orthopaedic specialist at Royal Prince Alfred Hospital, Sydney, never to have children as there was a one-in-three chance that they would inherit the disease.

By the time we left for Australia – in 1960 – David had left school and was studying medicine at Guy's Hospital in London. The rest of us packed our things and with feelings of misgiving, excitement, and, in my case, dread, set off for this strange new country on the other side of the world.

The trip began badly for me. I had a big collection of dolls and I packed as many as I could into a special case to take with me on the journey. At the train station while we were waiting to go to the port of Tilbury, the case sprang open and the dolls scattered everywhere. It seemed a bad omen.

My first impressions of Australia did nothing to improve things. I cried when I saw the scrawny trees with their miserable little leaves and scrappy-looking bark all falling off. They seemed so rubbishy after the lush English countryside I'd been used to. Father had chosen Armidale in the northern highlands of New South Wales. We moved into a house in town which was much bigger than the one we had left in England, and Father got a job at an orchard so he could learn about Australian agriculture. Two years after arriving in Armidale, he bought an orchard of his own at nearby Uralla.

George had left home and started work, so the remaining six children enrolled at a local public school. I shared a room with Pauline, who is eighteen months younger than me. We squabbled a lot, as sisters do. One point of difference was my messiness. I've always been untidy whereas Pauline is, if anything, excessively neat. I'm afraid I haven't improved with age in this department. Whenever I cook I leave a great mess everywhere. It doesn't worry me, but I know it can drive other people mad. Despite this difference and the inevitable competition between two sisters close in age, we got on reasonably well. We managed to study hard in the same room for our exams without actually coming to blows.

My schoolfriends in these early teenage years seemed interested mainly in pop music and boys. I liked music myself and owned a few records. I was friends with plenty of boys too, but I was only interested in larking about, nothing else. I didn't care about going to dances, either, which were all the rage. I just didn't share my friends' breathless enthusiasm for romance, real or imagined.

When I was fifteen I had one of the defining experiences of my life. My family was, of course, closely involved with our local church. A youth group from Sydney came to spend a week in Uralla, and two of them stayed on our farm. They were a bit older than me. We had many conversations about faith, and I began seriously to think about what it means to be a Christian. One day there was a meeting at the church involving this group. When it ended, the minister asked people to come down to the front and declare themselves for Christ. Pauline and I both rose to our feet and went forward. It was an emotional experience for me. All my life I'd obeyed my father and observed the ritual of church on Sunday. As a child I'd been hit across the knuckles for talking in church. This was different. It was at this moment that I decided that I would actually live according to Christian principles. This relationship with Christ has never left me.

I used to knock about with a group of four girls at school. We all had big plans for the future. We were going to complete Year Twelve and then go on to university together. I wanted to be a doctor. One day at the end of Year Ten, my father pulled me aside and told me that now I had completed my exams I would be leaving home.

We were standing in the yard outside the kitchen window. I can picture the scene now: my father's face stern as he made his announcement. I felt as though the ground had fallen away underneath me. 'What?' I said. 'I want to matriculate.'

'No. You have three younger sisters to consider. How do you think I'm going to feed and pay for them?'

I told him that I dreamed of being a doctor. David was already a doctor. I didn't claim to be as smart as him, but I promised I'd work hard and do my schoolwork and achieve. George was visiting us at the time and I enlisted his support, but our arguments made no difference. 'No,' Father said again. 'You're a very selfish girl. You should consider your younger sisters.'

I knew that once he'd made up his mind, nothing would change it. I just had to accept that this was one dream that was never going to come true.

It was decided that as Mother had been a children's nurse, that would be good enough for me. Mother and I took the train to Sydney to enrol me at the Royal Alexandra Hospital for Children at Camperdown. When I was presented to the matron, she said she'd never had such a young student. I was really too young to enrol but as I was turning seventeen in March, the month they were starting training, they accepted me.

When the time came for me to go to Sydney to live, my father gave me money for the train ticket with instructions that I was to repay him when I earned a salary. I had to pay board and lodging of a guinea a week at the nurses' home. It was eight weeks before I received my first pay packet. Father had not given me any pocket money, so I did it hard. I was so poor that I even had to borrow toothpaste from my housemates.

I paid my father back the train fare but did not return home for six months. I was confused and upset. I wondered what I had done wrong. What crime had I committed just to be thrown out like that? In hindsight, I can see that my father was probably barely making a living from the orchard. Mother had a stand beside the road from which she used to sell her home-made apple jelly. When I think about it now it was pathetic, really, but at the time I never realised how tough things were.

Rosemary persuaded me that I should try not to hold a grudge. I did my best but I am sure that this business is why I started operating outside the traditional conservative background in which I had been brought up. In the beginning, it was a matter of survival. At the age of sixteen I was making all the decisions about my life alone. I had to grow up fast.

As disgruntled as I was to begin with, I soon began to enjoy my independence. I'm naturally outspoken. I find it hard to hold my tongue if I see an injustice or if I disagree with something. I've also got a short temper. I blow up easily and tend to do a lot of shouting, but once I've let off steam I carry on as usual. I'd always had to suppress that side of my character at home. Now I was free to be myself at last.

American soldiers from the Vietnam War were coming to Australia on rest and recreation leave. My fellow students in the nurses' home used to go to nightclubs and discos at Kings Cross to meet them, but my social life revolved mainly around St Barnabas Church, in the inner city. St Barnabas was the Sydney University church so there were plenty of young people in the congregation. I soon found myself leading the youth group, organising social events and outings – my bossy personality coming out, I suppose. I was enjoying life. I had good friends and I was loving working with children.

At St Barnabas I met the young woman who would share my first African adventure, and who would become a lifelong friend. Rowene Brooker was also a nurse at the children's hospital, living with relatives while she studied. I was a year ahead of her and we didn't meet until we had both graduated. Sharing the same interest in paediatrics and both being active in the youth group, we soon became good friends. We were all set to rent a flat together when, one Sunday at church, Rowene came up to me and said, 'How would you like to rent a flat in Ethiopia instead?'

It was 1973. Ethiopia was in the grip of a devastating famine. No one in the rest of the world had heard about it until a BBC reporter, Jonathan Dimbleby, broadcast a documentary. It showed heartrending images of starving, fly-covered children waiting hopelessly to die. Nursing mothers with dried-up breasts stared listlessly at the camera, too weak even to beg. By the time these scenes had been shown, 100,000 people had already died. The western world had reacted with a rush of aid, but before the drought was over, more than 200,000 would perish and another million would be brought to ruin.

Rowene and I were only vaguely aware of all this. Unbeknown to either of us, a friend of Rowene's whose father, John Neil, represented the Sudan Interior Mission in Australia (SIM), had put Rowene's name and mine forward as possible volunteers to help with the famine. In addition to missionary activities, SIM was involved with aid. When Mr Neil rang Rowene, she wasn't too keen. She had thought she might do some kind of missionary work at some time, but for the moment she was having too much fun in Australia. Nevertheless, she decided she'd see what I thought.

I told her what I thought, all right. I was furious at her friend for putting forward my name without asking. When I'd cooled down a bit we talked about it. Some of Rowene's friends had already told her she'd be mad to pass up such an opportunity for adventure. In the end, my whole motivation for going was to look after Rowene. I must have been such a bighead. I thought, she's too young and shy to look after herself. If there's any trouble, I can stand up for her and help her out. Never mind that I was a year younger than Rowene and completely unworldly myself.

Once we had decided to go, the SIM people wanted us in Ethiopia as soon as possible. There was a lot to do to get ready. We went on Rowene's motorbike to the Ethiopian consulate – in Vaucluse, I think it was. We had to have a series of vaccinations against a whole host of exotic diseases. The one for typhus was especially hard to find; we spent an entire day running around town looking for somewhere that stocked the vaccine. I needed a trip to the dentist and I had to make a quick visit to Uralla to say goodbye to my parents.

Mother was doing the ironing when I broke the news that I was going to Ethiopia. 'That's nice, dear,' she said. 'I hope you have a lovely time.'

Father was in his office downstairs. He called up, 'Did the girl say she's going to Ethiopia, Barbara?'

'Yes, Val's off to Ethiopia.'

There was silence. A few minutes later, he appeared holding a world atlas. He put it on the ironing board and opened it out at a map of Africa. 'I don't think you understand, Barbara. Ethiopia's in the middle of Africa.'

'It can't be. There are lions there that eat people, aren't there?'

'She can't go.'

I said, 'The ticket's bought, so what am I supposed to do?'

'You've got no visa.'

'I've got it.'

'How?'

'Because I've got Australian citizenship.'

Father was speechless. There was an incredulous look on his face. After a few moments, he said, 'You go down to my study and call the British Embassy this minute and apologise. This is disgusting. I'll pay for the phone call.'

I said, 'I'm not going to do that. I've got an Australian passport and I'm ready to fly.'

'Outrageous. No one in this family renounces British citizenship.'

'Well, I have. I went down to the government offices at Chifley Square and filled out the papers.'

After that, whenever anyone from our family became an Australian citizen, he'd say to them, 'You've been talking to Valerie, haven't you?' Father never changed his citizenship and he forbade my mother to do so as well. When my aunt, her sister, became an Australian citizen, he could hardly believe it. 'She's gone crazy,' he said.

Twelve days after Rowene and I had agreed to go, we boarded an Alitalia flight for Bombay, our first stopover.

Looking back now I realise that we had absolutely no mental

preparation for what lay ahead. I remember sitting on the plane and telling Rowene, 'Do you realise that this place we're going to is in Africa? The people must be black.'

'What?'

'Black people. We've been looking after whites; can you imagine what this is going to be like?'

'I hope they're not going to ask us to wash them.'

'They might,' I said. 'We *are* nurses.'

I was 22, Rowene was 23. We were hopelessly young and naïve. We knew nothing about the world outside our own cosseted existence. We were about to grow up very fast.

CHAPTER 2

The Ethiopian Airlines flight lurched in the thermals rising from the baking ground below, then banked unsteadily to line up the runway. Peering through my little window, I could see, shimmering in the heat haze, serried ranks of hills which surround Addis Ababa like a natural barrier. As we descended, clusters of conical thatched roofs were revealed, scattered across burnt, brown countryside. Toy animals meandered along the roads while toy cars weaved amongst them. In the distance, the glint of sun on corrugated iron marked the city. Actually, it was more of a big town than a city; there seemed to be no high-rise buildings at all. Suddenly the landscape was rushing by, the plane hit the ground heavily, and the engines screamed a welcome.

The director of SIM in Addis Ababa, Mr Stilwell, and his wife, greeted us in the shabby terminal building and ushered us outside to a four-wheel-drive vehicle driven by an Ethiopian man. They didn't introduce us. There seemed to be no road rules or, if there were, they were of a kind that I couldn't understand. Our driver proceeded with one hand on the horn, bullying more cautious cars out of the way. Pedestrians, too, were shown no quarter. The rival traffic consisted mostly of beaten-up vehicles, belching black smoke as they rattled over pockmarked roads. Leather-faced men, draped in grubby *garbis*, a sort of all-purpose blanket, and carrying sturdy staffs, urged herds of goats and cattle through the melee. We passed a big building surrounded by fenced yards, with vultures roosting in rows along the roofline. Mr Stilwell told us this was the abattoir where the animals were going to be slaughtered. Occasionally when we stopped, beggars, some with terrible deformities, or women with children or carrying babies, stood silently beside the windows and held out their hands for alms. Our hosts kept the windows firmly closed.

The Stilwells lived in a comfortable house in what I suppose was a typical middle-class suburb, although I'd never before seen a home surrounded by high walls with a guard on the gate. They showed us into a bedroom, which we were to share. After showering, we sat down for a briefing.

Right from the beginning there was trouble.

In Sydney we had been told we would be working either at the public hospital in Addis – the Black Lion – or in the country with a medical team which was already well established. Mr Stilwell now informed us that we *were* the medical team. And we'd be going to the south of the country to relieve another team which was being sent to the famine area.

Our first impressions had already made us apprehensive. Being told that we were going alone into the wilds of the countryside seemed crazy. I told Mr Stilwell that we were not a medical team, we were just a couple of nurses who had only recently graduated. We didn't have the qualifications he needed. We certainly weren't equipped to run a clinic by ourselves in the middle of nowhere in a third-world country.

The SIM was a Baptist organisation with a strictly fundamentalist view of the world and I guess Mr Stilwell wasn't used to being challenged by a young upstart. I suggested that we'd be happy to work at the Black Lion, but he insisted that we had to do what we were told. It was like talking to my father except this time I wasn't afraid to answer back.

Things got a little heated. At one stage I threatened that Rowene and I would catch the first plane home. We argued back and forth for a while but it ended in a stalemate. As there was nothing further we could do that day, we ate a meal together, making brittle conversation, then went early to bed.

By next day I'd cooled down and both of us were feeling a little more courageous. Rowene and I talked it out and decided that, since we were here, we might as well try to do as they asked. But then Mr Stilwell came up with something else for us to think about. It had been decided that the current medical team would stay in the south, and Rowene and I would go north to Alamata, into the heart of the famine.

We spent the next two days looking for equipment to take with us. In the market we bought camping gear, including a tent, a couple of folding beds, a two-burner Primus stove and pots and pans. Mrs Stilwell told us that the nurse's uniforms we had brought with us were too short – the Ethiopians would be scandalised by our bare legs – so we bought some material to make into trousers when we got a chance.

Shortly after dawn we bundled our stuff into the SIM vehicle and, still with some trepidation, set off on an all-day drive north. The SIM compound in Alamata had an office, a clinic, a school and a feeding station where they distributed food aid. There were a couple of houses where European missionaries lived. There was a cattle adviser from Queensland, an agricul-turalist from Adelaide, a married couple who wanted to work with SIM, and a couple of doctors who were always moving around.

We were billeted in the house of the administrator, Mr Radich, and his wife. They were Americans, with two children who were at boarding school back home. In another house there was a Canadian pharmacist, Mr Leowen, and his wife. They had two young children who lived with them. I don't know the Leowens' first names. We always addressed them as Mr or Mrs – they were very particular about that.

The famine in this part of the country was just about under control by now. SIM was still feeding a few hundred people every day, housed in a yard surrounded by a high wire fence. Each day before they were fed, someone would have to go in and remove the bodies of those who had died overnight. As feeding time approached, the people would rattle the wire like animals in a zoo, then mission staff would bring out big pots of gluey, grey porridge for them to eat. It was the most horrible, dehumanising thing I had ever seen.

It was decided that Rowene and I would go out into the countryside to assess how the small communities were faring. We were also expected to preach the gospel. The people in this area were predominantly Coptic Christians.

Being the only permanent member of the SIM compound with medical knowledge, Mr Leowen was our immediate boss. He gave us a rundown on the local diseases that we could expect to encounter. As he began to go through a long list of chest complaints, diarrhoea, internal parasites, typhus and so on, I could feel my temper rising. By the time he reached malaria, I could no longer keep quiet. I burst out: 'This is crazy. We only know about malaria by looking it up in the dictionary. We haven't got anything like the knowledge we need to work here. Look, we're happy to work in the Black Lion in Addis and replace nurses there, but we're just not prepared for this.'

Mr Leowen was a big man. I'm short and slightly built. Towering over me, he growled: 'Whatever gave you this idea? It's not your place to talk like this. We've organised this, not you. You'll do what you're told.'

It was a real personality clash – I couldn't stand his domineering manner. I drew myself up to my full height, about level with his stomach, and argued right back. We had a full and frank discussion for a while, but in the end it was obvious that I was never going to win. We finally agreed that next day we'd give it a try.

That night Rowene and I ate our dinner with the Radiches. Mrs Radich said: 'You'd better both have baths, they'll be the last you get for a long while.'

In the morning we loaded our equipment onto a couple of donkeys and set off for a village called Bala, situated in a river valley about 30 kilometres away. It was a day-long trek down a steep escarpment. With us were Mr Leowen and two interpreters. Tadesse was a nineteen-year-old boy from Eritrea. He had been educated at a SIM school. Since the Ethiopian emperor, Haile Selassie, had annexed Eritrea in 1962, the country had been engaged in a murderous war with Ethiopia. As the schools had all closed, some English-speaking students had been brought down to act as interpreters. The other was a bush boy, Asghedom, who was from Tigray province. His English was not so good.

An American doctor, Dr Barlow, had already been in Bala for four days with his wife preparing for our arrival. He'd rented a big hut to use as a clinic and one of the ubiquitous circular huts, or *tukuls*, for us to cook and sleep in.

The first night we were there I got a further insight into the archaic workings of the Sudan Interior Mission. Mrs Barlow cooked dinner. I expected that Tadesse and Asghedom would sit down and eat with us, but instead they were sent off to the village to find their own food. There were no shops, so they would have had to scrounge from the local people or else go hungry. When I remarked on this, Mr Leowen gave us a long lecture about fraternising with the local people. He had made up a list of nine rules which we were expected to obey. I can't remember all of them but they included such things as not sharing meals with indigenous workers, not socialising with them after working hours, never being alone with a male, and so on. The mission seemed to think that because they were Africans they were lesser beings. Needless to say, when the Barlows and Mr Leowen left a couple of days later, we happily disobeyed every one of these rules. Tadesse and Asghedom, and other locals with whom we worked, became good friends.

The people of Bala suffered from a range of ailments which we had never encountered in Australia. About a hundred people would come to the clinic each day, many of them having walked long distances. Malaria was a big problem, and tuberculosis was common. Sometimes the best that Rowene and I could do was take a guess at what was wrong. We were often completely out of our depth, and could only hope and pray that our treatment was doing some good.

One day a man of about 35 or 40 was brought in by his relatives from out in the country. He had severe watery diarrhoea and was lapsing in and out of consciousness. We diagnosed typhoid fever, put him on six-hourly doses of Chloranphenicol and placed him in a separate hut away from the clinic. Although we had some electrolyte for rehydration, neither Rowene nor I was trained at inserting canulas, so we had to administer it orally, which was frustrating. For two days we fought for his life. His relatives, I think, were quite bemused that we were making such an effort. I've often seen since in Africa that when someone is extremely ill they become resigned to their death and just stop treatment. Perhaps it's not such a bad idea.

Rowene and I took it in turns to watch him through the night. On the third day he suddenly went into cardiac arrest. Rowene began cardiac resuscitation while I did mouth-to-mouth. He vomited a couple of times and I got a mouthful of stomach contents. In the end, we lost the battle and he died. The relatives were not only amazed but terribly grateful that we had tried so hard.

I still find it bizarre that the mission sent two raw young nurses into the field like this. Thirty years later, after having seen many times how some missionaries behave in Africa, I can surmise that they were really more interested in us saving souls than lives. We did pray over people who were dying, but we never preached to them. I think that our actions were the best form of preaching. In fact, I still firmly believe that the best way to convince people about the love of God is by actions, not words.

Almost daily we'd find ourselves fighting to save someone's life. A boy baby of about six or eight weeks old came in with severe diarrhoea. We gave him the appropriate antibiotics and sent him home with his parents. They didn't give him any fluids, and a day later he came back very dehydrated. As it happened, there was a SIM doctor visiting. He put a subcutaneous needle into the abdomen and started a drip, but it was too late and the baby died.

Another case which sticks in my mind was that of a little girl who had fallen into a fire. She was burnt all down her front. We treated her as for open burns: we broke open ampoules of antibiotic and sprinkled them directly onto her injuries, and antibiotic powder as well. She wasn't urinating, so we gave her lots of tea. After a while, she started urinating again, which made us feel more hopeful. We borrowed a big basket from one of the locals and put her in it with a cloth over her to keep the flies off. I had sent a message to Alamata about the girl, and a day later a helicopter arrived to take her to a proper hospital. And, by the grace of God, she lived.

Everything had to be done through our interpreters. It was sometimes maddening that we just didn't seem to be on the same wavelength as the people we were trying to treat. One woman came in bleeding heavily after having given birth prematurely. Obstetrics was one thing that we did know about but she wouldn't let us give her Ergometrine, which makes the muscles of the uterus contract. She knew to cross her legs, which is one of the things done for this type of bleeding. After a lot of persuasion, she allowed Rowene to rub the fundus. You tickle the top of the uterus through the tummy, which makes it contract and stop haemorrhaging. This woman, too, was one of our successes.

Some of our patients were distrustful, which often compromised the care we would have liked to give. Later, back in Alamata, a woman arrived after being in labour for three days. She had somehow managed to walk for a day to get there. There was an English midwife in the clinic who was more experienced than either of us. She diagnosed a face presentation, whereby the baby is coming face first, instead of with the top of the head first, and can get stuck in the birth canal. She suggested to the woman's family that they take her to the hospital at Dessie, an hour's drive away. A truck was standing by to take her. Although she was in terrible pain, she and her husband said no. We moved her into a side room and, a few hours later, she died.

Despite the harsh conditions and often distressing work, Rowene and I got on well together. We were different enough to complement one another. Rowene was easygoing and understanding, and I've always been able to go to sleep instantly when I need to. If we had a patient who needed treatment overnight, I'd usually be the one to get up and give the injection or whatever. Rowene was not a good sleeper. She was the one who did most of the cooking.

We'd brought some European food with us from Alamata. When it ran out, we resorted to local food; there was still some available, as Bala had never been in the worst part of the famine area. Rowene made stews of goat and chicken. We were able to buy onions and spices in the village, and vegetables now and again. Sometimes the villagers gave us some of the Ethiopian staple, *injera*, a flat, rubbery sort of pancake made from a special wheat, *tef*. They grind it up, mix it with water and let it ferment for a while before cooking it on a flat plate. Breakfast was *ambasha* – unleavened bread which we made ourselves – lentils and tea. The two boys shared all of our meals.

We all used to lark around sometimes to relax. Once when we had finished seeing patients for the day, I squirted water from a syringe over Tadesse. He squirted me back and, before we knew it, the four of us were engaged in a water fight which ended with us all falling about with laughter. The villagers must have heard about our mad behaviour because next day when I was out walking, some girls threw water at me and ran away giggling.

The locals were fascinated by Rowene's flaming red hair. Everywhere she went, it attracted attention, to the point where she sometimes became exasperated. Some young women persuaded her one day to allow them to plait it into the long corn rows that they wear. Rowene sat with them for hours while they patiently worked away. She ran out of time when they were only half finished, so she promised to go back next day to complete the job. That night she woke me up saying she had a terrible headache caused by the tight plaiting. I spent a couple of hours undoing all their careful work. I think they were quite disappointed the next day when Rowene told them she was cancelling the rest of her hair appointment.

*

After six weeks in Bala we started running out of things to do. We decided to walk back to Alamata to see if they would send us somewhere else. It was good timing, because there was an outbreak of typhus at a small town called Gubgubdu, 30 kilometres away. An Australian nurse who had been working there had contracted the disease and been brought in to Alamata close to death. They'd only just managed to save her.

We were glad then that we'd gone to such trouble searching Sydney for the typhus vaccine. We'd brought our follow-up doses with us. When we went to take them, Mr Leowen told us that they were useless! They were for a different strain from the one in Ethiopia.

Even after working with them so closely, we were still expected to treat Tadesse and Asghedom like servants. When the day's work was done, they used to join their friends in the town to drink tea and talk. Rowene and I would go for a walk to town and 'just happen' to run into them. The gates of the compound were closed at ten o'clock. Once or twice when we came back after curfew, we had to sneak across a cactus field and climb over the back wall. It was all very silly. Here we were, two young women in our early twenties, and we were treated as though we were thirteen-year-olds. Fortunately, our evil deeds were never discovered.

The day before we were due to leave for Gubgubdu, Rowene fell down and hurt her ankle. The doctor at the clinic suspected that it might be broken and suggested that she go to the hospital at Dessie where they had an x-ray machine. Mr Radich refused to let her go, as she would have had to be driven by a man and there would be just the two of them in the car. So, the doctor bound her foot tightly and told her to keep the weight off it. Rowene's place was taken by an English nurse called Pat.

Rowene and I both said goodbye to Asghedom, whose place was being taken by Samuel, a young man from Eritrea, who spoke something like six languages. Like Asghedom, he would become a good pal as well as a colleague.

Gubgubdu was my first visit to an Afar area. The fact hardly registered with me at the time because we were in the midst of a full-blown typhus epidemic. It's a wicked disease. It inflames the blood vessels, and sufferers experience severe headache, fever and low blood pressure. If it's not treated, the blood may stop pumping and the patient will die. It isn't always fatal, but if you're a bit run-down, as most people are in Ethiopia, it can be a killer.

We saved a lot of patients with Tetracyclin, but there were some whom we did not save. On one awful day a mother lost three children. In the morning she brought a sick girl child to me; while I was examining her, she died on my lap. At midday another of this woman's children died and, at the end of the day, another. Three children in one day. I found it hard to believe that existence could be like that. I came from a good safe home where the possibility of children dying through disease and malnutrition was unthinkable. I had just finished training in a hospital with an intensive care ward boasting all the equipment to save children's lives you could want. I was such an innocent. For the first time in my life, I realised that there were glaring inequalities in the world. This revelation filled me with anger. I wished that I could change things, but the injustice was so great and so widespread that I wondered what difference one person could make.

It took three weeks to get the epidemic under control. When I returned to Alamata they told us they had another assignment for us. Rowene and I were to travel north to Afdera in an area known as the Danakil Depression. It's one of the lowest and hottest places on earth; 120 metres below sea level in parts. Summer temperatures can reach 50 degrees Celsius. The landscape is largely stony desert with a sparse scattering of thorn bushes and acacia trees. Living in this inhospitable place are a people who are as tough as their environment – the Danakil or, as they prefer to be called today, Afar.

When they heard where we were going, some highland people warned us that these Afar were a fierce, warlike people who did not like foreigners and placed great store on toughness and bravery. The weak did not survive in the Danakil desert. The highland people said that, in the past, one of the requirements for manhood was to kill and castrate a member of an enemy tribe. The young Afar man was then looked upon with respect and entitled to various rights, such as marriage. One person went so far as to predict that we would certainly be killed! And, in case that wasn't enough to frighten us, they pointed out that the Afar were almost universally Muslim and women had no rights.

I shall have something to say about these stories later. Suffice to say that, for two young girls from Australia, there were plenty of misgivings about what lay ahead.

Rowene, Tadesse, Samuel, Mr Radich and I flew to Afdera in the mission's single-engine plane. After he let us off, Bob the pilot made another trip to bring some of our gear. We had planned to set up with a week's supply of medicine and food. What we couldn't fit into the plane was due to arrive two days later by camel.

Mr Radich had already arranged everything with the clan leader. They'd prepared an area of desert for an airstrip and built a large hut out of sticks for us to use as a clinic. The sticks had not yet been plastered with the usual mud mixed with straw, so the wind blew straight through, but there was a roof.

Afar nomads live in small, dome-shaped dwellings called *deboitas*, about 3 metres wide and a metre and a half high. They're made from a framework of sticks covered with matting made out of dried palm leaf fronds. When the pasture runs out and it's time for the Afar to move on, they dismantle their homes and load them onto their camels. By contrast, our clinic, with three separate rooms, was positively luxurious. Mr Radich asked the chief why he'd built such a big hut for us. 'Now that we've got an airport,' he said, 'we'll get lots of visitors. After you leave, this can be the terminal building.'

After seeing us settled in, Mr Radich said goodbye and left us to it. That night, Rowene and I slept in our tent, while Tadesse and Samuel happily slept in the open. Next day about a hundred people attended our first clinic. I don't know where they all came from or how they heard about it out there in the desert, but there was never any shortage of patients. Most of them were suffering from malaria. There weren't as many desperately ill people as we'd seen in the highlands because there weren't many flies and fleas in the desert.

The Afar women were beautiful – tall and slim, with fine features and glowing black skin. They wore long, flowing dresses and many of them wore nothing on top. Unmarried women wore a head covering made from hundreds of tiny, brightly coloured plastic beads strung together.

The men wore a short sarong called a *foota*. They went about bare-chested with a shawl thrown loosely over their shoulders. Many wore a necklace strung with a row of little leather pouches, within which were pieces of paper with sayings from the Koran. Most carried a large curved knife at their waist and quite a few carried rifles. Their hair was long and arranged in a multitude of corkscrew curls. They twist it around a stick then set it with a solution made from a crushed vine. It's then dressed with clarified butter. It ends up a metallic, greyish colour. The young men showed no curiosity about us. They were proud, self-contained, haughty.

Far from being bloodthirsty and hostile, the Afar were incredibly hospitable. After we'd been there a couple of days, the chief came to see how we were getting on. He brought with him a kid, which, thank goodness, someone else killed for us. We were invited to watch the people dance.

The main diet of the Afar was bread – *ga'ambo* – and fresh milk from camels, goats, sheep or cattle, or else, fermented yoghurt, *itiha*. There was also a kind of porridge they made out of dura flour which comes from sorghum and is laboriously ground by hand. Milk is so important that it has ceremonial uses and on social occasions, a camel's stomach containing fresh camel's milk was passed around. You tilted it up and squirted the milk into your mouth rather as you would with a Spanish wineskin. I liked camel's milk immediately. It was different from cow's milk and stronger than goat's.

The chief had appointed two guards to watch over us and one of them was obviously a bit keen on Rowene. But as soon as she made it clear she wasn't interested, he backed off and treated us with respect. In fact, in all of our time in Afdera, we had not a hint of trouble from men. All the warnings about Muslim males proved completely false.

After a few days, our supply of water, which was stored in plastic jerrycans, started running low. We weren't at all keen on having to go with the women to the nearest well, as it was an hour's walk away. We hit upon the idea of charging a cup of water for consultations. The Afar were only too happy with this arrangement and we ended up with as much water as we needed. There was even enough for Rowene to wash her hair.

After a week or so, our supplies of medicine were beginning to run low. We had been in Ethiopia for nearly three months and were due to be flown out of Afdera any day, as we had planned to return to Australia on 6 March 1974. On 28 February we heard a radio broadcast on the BBC World Service which threw our future into question. There were strong rumours that a coup was imminent.

For the last 44 years, Ethiopia had been a feudal society ruled by the emperor, Haile Selassie. For months, there had been simmering unrest, fuelled by a group of army officers who wanted to sweep away the antiquated system. There were outbreaks of fighting all over, throwing the country into confusion. Shortly after we left, Haile Selassie would be overthrown. The new leader was an army officer, Major Mengistu.

In the meantime, we had no way of communicating with SIM headquarters or of knowing how this would affect us. In Addis the airport was closed and all aircraft had been grounded. The SIM people were trying frantically to get permission to send their plane to rescue us. If that failed, they were working on an alternative plan to send in a camel team to pick us up and take us across the desert to Assab on the Eritrean coast. After a couple of days they were granted permission to fetch us. The SIM plane was the only one in the entire country which was allowed to fly.

When Bob landed in Afdera and told us we were to return to Addis, we had very mixed feelings. We were only now getting used to Ethiopia. After our shaky beginning, we felt that we were working effectively. It seemed a waste of that hard-learned experience to send us home.

At Alamata, the Radiches had packed up our belongings and had them waiting on the airstrip when we landed. They told us that most expatriates were quitting the country, and it would be wise for us to do the same. Using the plane's radio, we pleaded with Mr Stilwell in Addis to be allowed to stay. I realise now that we must have seemed ungrateful. They had gone to great lengths to get us out of there and now we were refusing to go. How young and thoughtless we were.

Mr Stilwell insisted that we were to go to Addis, where we would regroup and plan what to do next. Bob refuelled the plane, using one of Rowene's petticoats to strain the fuel, and we set off.

When we landed, the airport was eerily quiet. Nothing was moving. The city streets were practically deserted except for tanks and military vehicles. There were soldiers on guard outside all the government buildings. We passed through three checkpoints on the way to SIM headquarters.

It turned out that Mr Stilwell was not at all inflexible about sending us home. He had just been worried about us out there in the middle of the desert and wanted us in Addis to sort things out. After four days it seemed that life in the capital was returning to normal. We still didn't know much about the rebels or what their aims were. There were rumours that they were Communists and that they wanted to change the entire structure of Ethiopian society. I'm ashamed to say that this didn't make much impression on me at the time; I was more interested in the immediate problem of getting back to work. It was only later that I would realise the full extent of the hardships that were about to be visited on the country that I was beginning to love.

SIM had medical and food supplies waiting to be sent north. When the truck left at four in the morning, Rowene and I were aboard. A few days later we found ourselves once again in Afar country with Tadesse and Samuel, running a clinic in a little town called Ibiidi.

Ibiidi was in the *woreda*, or district, of Teeru. The Sultan of Teeru, a very regal man who dressed always in flowing robes and a turban of pure white, had our hut built immediately below his own home. He detailed a guard to watch over us, and called often with gifts of water and milk. He always asked politely if we had slept well and if there was anything we needed. He was a lovely old man, a little puzzled, I think, by our single status. He told me quietly one day that because he liked me he would give me one of his men to marry. I thanked him for his kind offer and respectfully declined.

The Sultan's subjects, too, showed us typically generous Afar hospitality. At social gatherings, they sometimes showed off their dancing skills. Afar dancing is very dramatic. The men, holding knives and sticks, stand in one spot and jump up and down. It's a competition of manliness. They push their bodies harder and harder, jumping higher and higher. The women dance in lines. They call out to the men, strange, melodious cries which come from the back of the throat, and the men answer them. Each dance tells a story, rather like the corroborees of Australian Aboriginal people. We showed them a few moves ourselves. It was all good innocent fun, but it got us into trouble later. I can remember those first Afar dancers vividly. I can see their faces, they made such an impression on me.

I've since been back to Gubgubdu many times. It's called Yallo in Afar and it's grown into a big market village. I've seen again where we lived and worked. In Teeru, I've met people who say they knew me as far back as that first visit. It's a funny thing that most of my first trip to Ethiopia is a blur, but the Afar part has remained in my memory as clearly as if it were yesterday.

The remaining three months of our stay in Ethiopia flew by quickly. On the morning that Rowene and I were to leave the SIM compound we had breakfast with a group of Ethiopian and

Eritrean friends. They each made a short speech, and, without a trace of embarrassment, each sang us a little song. Rowene made a tape recording which she treasures to this day. Here is what Tadesse said:

'Val and Rowene, it was good enjoying all the good times we had out here. We really appreciate you, and I know we're going to miss you a lot. But it's all right, because you're going back to where you belong – home sweet home.'

Tadesse sang a beautiful song about Jesus' love for mankind. Then our friends together sang 'Auld Lang Syne' in Amharic, the principal language of Ethiopia. These were the boys with whom we had shared our successes and failures over the last six months. We had laughed and cried with them; worked, played, argued and worshipped together. They were more than colleagues, more than friends; they had become brothers. As we walked away, I reflected on what Tadesse had said. I was no longer certain that Australia *was* my home.

CHAPTER 3

The SIM representative, Mr Neil, was waiting at Sydney Airport when we arrived. He wanted us to go with him immediately for a debriefing. We were tired and jet-lagged. We suggested that we make a time on the following day, but no, it had to be now. When we sat down in his office, the reason for his insistence became clear. He had received unfavourable reports from Addis Ababa about our behaviour. We had fraternised shamelessly with the local people and given them too much responsibility at work. For instance, we had allowed Samuel to look after the servicing of a motor vehicle – never mind that neither Rowene nor I knew the first thing about cars. One of our worst crimes had been that we'd danced with our friends in Teeru. We were not the sort of people, said Mr Neil, whom SIM would wish to employ.

By then I'd listened long enough. I told him just what I thought about SIM's policies and ended up declaring that we wouldn't want to work for them either.

That difficult beginning set the tone for our homecoming. Rowene and I were haunted by the poverty and injustice we had witnessed in Ethiopia. Everything in Australia seemed rich and bloated; people were oblivious to life out there in the developing world, where each day was a struggle for existence. We both wanted to get back to Africa as soon as possible. We wrote and telephoned aid agencies and humanitarian groups offering our services. The answer was always the same. The war with Eritrea had become worse and the new military regime, the *Dergue*, was tearing Ethiopia apart, trying to turn it into a Marxist state. People who opposed them were being killed or thrown into prison. Religious worship had been banned, churches were closed, missionaries were being deported and, in some cases, murdered. No one wanted to send us into danger.

At first our friends enjoyed hearing all about our adventures. The trouble was, though, we could talk about nothing else. We couldn't get Ethiopia out of our heads. After a while they grew tired of it and began avoiding us.

Although we couldn't get back to Africa, Rowene and I had success helping some of our friends to come to Australia. Under the law then, if they had a place to stay, had been accepted by a school or university and had their return fare paid, they could come as sponsored students. Tadesse arrived first. Rowene and I paid his fare, and Rowene went guarantor for him. He was followed by three more Eritrean boys. Tadesse ended up becoming an Australian citizen. We would have liked to help Samuel, too, but by then he was one of the thousands of young men who had been killed in the war.

After many months of frustration, we realised that we had no choice but to settle back into western society. Rowene and I had found jobs as nurses at the Sydney Eye Hospital. We rented a flat in Glebe with two other girls, who had absolutely no interest in missionary work or third-world poverty, and tried to forget about what we had been through. It was difficult, but over the next couple of years I began to put my Ethiopian experience behind me. Admittedly, Rowene and I still kept in touch with our

Eritrean friends but, on the whole, I was making a good fist of living a conventional Australian life – or, at least, I thought I was.

One day in late 1976, I received a telegram from a German organisation, Asme-Humanitas, offering me a job as a nurse in a refugee camp in Sudan near the Eritrean border. My first reaction was annoyance. I'd been through all this business of friends not accepting me, I was doing my best to fit back into normal society and now, just when I was starting to succeed, these people wanted to upset things. I threw the telegram in the bin.

A couple of days later I complained to Rowene and our Eritrean friends about it. One of the boys said, 'If that camp's near the Eritrean border, they're going to be Eritrean refugees. Why are you disregarding these people? They're our people. What sort of a person are you?'

'The sort of person who wants a chance,' I retorted. 'I've done my bit. I'm settling down now.'

'No,' he said. 'You should rethink that.'

The camp was called Wad el Hilaywa. And it *was* full of refugees fleeing from the upheavals in Eritrea. I found out later that an Eritrean friend, Eyob, whom I'd met in Alamata, had been working in the camp and had given my name to the leaders.

Two weeks after the first one, another telegram arrived. Asme-Humanitas were annoyed that I hadn't replied and asked me please to get in touch, giving me a telephone number in Germany. Tadesse offered to help me find the money to make a long-distance call. When I rang, I was all fired up to tell them to stop bothering me, but it turned out a bit differently from how I'd planned.

'We're desperate,' they said. 'If we don't find someone, we'll have to close the medical clinic. Could you just give us six months?'

Three weeks later I was on my way to Sudan.

*

Wad el Hilaywa was like a medium-sized town, except that it was fenced in and no one was allowed to enter or leave without permission. It was situated in a dried-up river valley within earshot of the Eritrean border. Acres and acres of tents and *tukuls* stretched as far as you could see, with a maze of narrow streets running between them. In the centre was a market. At night, you could sometimes hear the sounds of the war.

There was a Swedish-run clinic which specialised in caring for mothers, and children under five. They had a paediatrician, a couple of nurses and lots of modern equipment. For everyone else, there was the Asme-Humanitas clinic. As the only person with medical training, I was responsible for the health of 20,000 people. To assist me I had two surgical dressers, a couple of nurse aides, a mechanic to look after a rather beaten-up Land Rover, and someone to do the shopping and cooking. The whole operation was run by a very efficient English woman, Kirsty Wright, who was based in Khartoum, the capital. Strangely enough, I didn't feel at all daunted by the task ahead. It was a bit like being back in Bala, the first village we had worked at in Ethiopia, only many times bigger.

I slept on a camp bed in a corner of the medicine store. As early as three a.m., our assistant, Mohammad, would begin issuing numbers for those who wanted to attend clinic. The limit was 100 per day, and on most days every number was taken. At five, I'd light my charcoal fire and make tea, and then I'd go to visit patients who'd stayed in overnight. I'd dress injuries or administer medicine, or whatever needed to be done; then, at seven thirty, the rest of the staff would arrive and we'd open for business.

Each day there was a parade of people with TB, chest infections, eye and ear infections, all sorts of communicable diseases, injuries from accidents, malaria and some ailments that I could only guess at. The people came by donkey, they were carried in on stretchers, strapped onto camels, on foot . . . hardly ever by motor vehicle.

Few patients spoke English. My Arabic was passable, but I struggled with the other main language, Tigrinya. Sometimes communication became so muddled that the only thing to do was to break up with laughter. The patients were very good-humoured about my shortcomings.

At ten a.m. we'd stop for a short break and I'd have a breakfast of bread and tea. Then it was back into the fray until about two or three p.m. I'd snatch a quick lunch, then go to visit patients who were too sick to come to the clinic. It was always difficult to find them in the maze of the camp. In the evenings I'd have some *injera*, which was made from a different grain from the Ethiopian one, and was not quite as nice, and *suphee* (soup). Then I'd usually wander down to the market to drink tea under the flickering light of kerosene lanterns and chat with my colleagues.

One afternoon, when I was about to close the clinic, some people came in carrying a sick man on a camel. I told them to bring him back tomorrow morning; this camel was on heat. When they're like that they go quite mad and can be very dangerous. While they'd been talking to me, the camel literally bit the man's throat out. His friends rushed back and said, 'He's got no throat – will you treat him now?'

He was in a terrible state, bleeding heavily and struggling to breathe. I sent someone to fetch the Swedish doctor, Dr Greta, from the children's clinic while I did what I could to staunch the bleeding. We sewed him up as best we could, being careful not to block his airway. With a makeshift tube in his trachea, we bundled him into the Land Rover and drove him to Kasalla Hospital, 60 kilometres away, where they did a proper tracheotomy.

I went back to visit the man several times to see how he was getting on. He seemed to be recovering well, so I was stunned when I heard one day that he had died. You have to suck out tracheotomy patients regularly so that they don't choke on their own saliva. Instead of doing that, the night staff had gone to sleep. In Australia, there would have been an inquiry into such negligence. Here, people simply shrugged it off. It was just another small tragedy in a country that was full of them.

In the middle of 1977, about six months after I'd arrived, a patient who was one of the most distressing cases I'd ever seen came to the clinic. Halema was a vivacious and lively Eritrean woman from the Assowata tribe, who live on the Red Sea coast. Her husband was dead, and she had two small children, Fatuma, aged one and Abdela, three.

Poor Halema was riddled with TB. She had weeping sores all over her body and the infection had so affected the joints of her arms that she could barely move them. I started her on an intensive course of antibiotic therapy. She was in such a bad state, with no relatives nearby to care for her, that I had a little shelter built for her and her children beside the medical store where I slept.

My housegirl, Alem, was wonderful with the family. She cooked for them and looked after the children as if they were her own. I became very attached to the two little ones. They were such fun to be with that there were some days when I thought I'd just like to play with them instead of going to work.

Halema stayed with me for about a year, at the end of which I was in despair about ever being able to make her well again. At one stage, she left for a couple of months to try a traditional cure. When she came back, she was in an even worse state. I knew then that the outcome was inevitable. When she became so ill that I could no longer look after her, we took her to hospital. There she died. Some relatives were found, who took in Fatuma and Abdela.

*

The camp was an ideal breeding ground for trachoma, an insidious eye disease that is endemic in underdeveloped countries. Trachoma is caused by the bacteria *Chlamydia trachomatis*. It's spread easily on an infected person's hands or by flies which have come into contact with a sufferer. Wad el Hilaywa, with thousands of people crammed closely together, was rife with it.

I was aware that if trachoma were left untreated, the eyelashes would scratch the soft part of the eye, creating sores and eventually causing blindness. One of my medical textbooks described a simple operation which could be performed to prevent this. It involved cutting a small piece of flesh out of the eyelid, pulling the lid up, then stitching it so it would stay there. It didn't look too difficult, so I thought I'd give it a try.

The conditions were a bit tricky. We didn't have a proper operating theatre; an assistant had to keep waving the flies away, while another had to stop the relatives from coming too close and touching where we didn't want them to touch. But it worked. My trachoma operations proved to be so successful that soon I was doing two or three a day. Some of my repairs were pretty and some not so pretty, but we did prevent a lot of people from going blind.

It didn't take me long to realise that my German employer, Asme-Humanitas, was very disorganised. I often found that we were short of medicines; even when a shipment would finally arrive, it might have none of the stuff I'd ordered. Instead of vital medicine for such things as tuberculosis, they'd send me aspirin or vitamins or some such. This drove both Kirsty and me crazy.

I was still young enough to believe in simple solutions. I thought, here are lots of poor people who need assistance, surely all we have to do is find some rich person, tell them about this and they'll help. Kirsty was enough of an idealist to be fired up by this idea as well. She said she knew the ideal person, a wealthy Sudanese who had close connections to the government.

We made an appointment, and caught a taxi to his home. He lived in a mansion surrounded by manicured lawns that were highlighted by immaculate gardens, and hedges clipped into ornamental shapes. We walked up a flight of marble steps into a huge entrance hall. A servant showed us into a reception room to wait while he went to find his master. Beautiful alabaster ashtrays were scattered here and there. There were fifteen. We counted them.

Kirsty is from the East End of London. She has a PhD but you'd never know it; she's a bit of a larrikin, like me. She said, 'Hey, Val, let's pocket one of these.'

I told her I didn't think that was a good idea.

'Come on, this inlay's pure gold.'

'Let's just see how we go with him first.'

Before we had quite resolved the question, our host descended a curving staircase. He was wearing pure white Sudanese robes with a white cap on his head. He was one of the blackest men I've ever seen. He welcomed us in perfect Queen's English and asked what he could do for us.

Kirsty and I began telling him about the terrible plight of all these Eritrean refugees in the camp. Before we had gone very far, he interrupted. 'Ah yes, Eritrea. You know, I was fighting with Monty in the Second World War. We were in Eritrea. I thought we solved all of their problems. I don't know how they've got themselves into this pickle now.'

I'm repeating exactly what he said. Thousands of people were being killed, thousands more were fleeing across the border as refugees, and the Eritreans had 'got themselves into a pickle'.

I said, 'Yes, it is a pickle and we're trying to do something about it. We need money to buy medicine for tuberculosis. It's called Rifampicin.'

'Don't tell me you came to me for something so trifling. I know people in the Health Ministry, just give them my name.'

I said, 'I know that crazy ministry. I give them monthly health reports and they give me nothing. I'll get nothing from them.'

We played this little game for a while longer. In the end, he wrote down the name of someone in the ministry and ushered us out. It had been a complete waste of time. It was a good lesson, however, in human nature. I have seen many times since that it is often the rich who are most reluctant to part with a cent, while ordinary people will make sacrifices to help those in need.

Back at the camp I was commiserating with my colleagues about our failure. One of them said, 'You're the best trick in the whole pack of cards here. You're a foreigner. You can import anything you like, within reason. I could go to Port Sudan with your passport, buy some boxes of whisky and we could sell them and make a profit. Then we'd be able to buy our own medicine.'

It seemed like a good idea to me. Unfortunately, the President of Sudan, Mr Nimeiri, had just begun experimenting with Islamic law. He decided to give it a trial run in our province. The local police came to us and said that, under these new laws, they had to conduct a search.

'Not here,' I said. 'This is a clinic. There's only medicine here and a lot of sick people.'

They had obviously been tipped off because they insisted on searching every corner until, in the storehouse, they came across boxes and boxes of whisky.

'What are you doing with this?' asked the officer in charge.

'We're foreigners. We have to keep it here for medicinal purposes. It helps us sleep.'

'Is that so? And why would a woman need so many boxes?'

'I was afraid I might run out.'

They confiscated the cartons to hold as evidence until my trial. When the day came for my court appearance, I was suffering from a bout of malaria. I was feverish and shaking so much that my teeth were chattering. I must have looked as though I were shaking from fear. Fearful is putting it a bit strongly, but I admit that the thought of spending time in a Sudanese jail did make me quite nervous. The judge took only a few minutes to find me guilty of having alcohol in my possession. I don't know if my demeanour had anything to do with it, but I was given a suspended sentence and allowed to go free.

So we lost a lot of money and all of our whisky. I heard that the police who had arrested us were drunk for weeks afterwards.

After my run-in with the law, life in Wad el Hilaywa went on as usual. During the day, it was about 45 degrees in the shade. In direct sunlight, the thermometer went off the scale. Everyone complained, but I didn't find it too bad. I'd never been troubled by the heat, except that it was a nuisance being wet with perspiration all the time.

I lived without running water or electricity. In the evenings, there was very little to do except sit around chatting to my colleagues. They were all from Eritrea and were passionate about the independence struggle. As we sipped our tea under the flickering hurricane lanterns, I heard all about the long and ignoble history of Eritrea's exploitation, first by Italy and later by their neighbour, Ethiopia.

It had begun in 1840 when the Italian government bought up land at Assab on the Red Sea coast for the use of the national shipping company, Rubattino. As the European scramble for Africa gathered momentum, the Italians marched inland, subduing all opposition by force of arms. By 1889, they had taken Asmara, the capital, and were in firm control of the country. During the following decades of colonial rule, great swathes of land were taken from the local people and given to Italian settlers. On a political level, Eritreans were completely disenfranchised by being forbidden to work in the civil service.

Italy next turned her attention to Eritrea's neighbour, Ethiopia. The Italian armed forces forged south and by 1935 they were in control of the country. The Ethiopian monarch, Haile Selassie, had initially appealed for British help against the Italians but he had been shrugged off. Ethiopia was considered to be of no significance to Britain's interests. That attitude changed when Italy entered the Second World War on the side of Germany. Ethiopia was deemed suddenly to be strategically important. Where appeals to decency had failed, self-interest now prevailed. The British invaded, capturing Asmara in 1941, and liberating Eritrea and Ethiopia from the Italian colonisers. As the tide of the world war turned in the Allies' favour, they withdrew from Eritrea, leaving a country beset by high unemployment and urban unrest.

With the British gone, Eritrea's future was left in the balance. The British favoured partition, with the north and west going to Sudan and the rest to Ethiopia. Of course, Haile Selassie had no objection to that. In 1949, the UN established a commission of inquiry to find out what Eritreans wanted. The various parties could not agree and in the end it was the western powers, and in particular the United States, who decided Eritrea's fate. As usual, they were motivated by their own strategic interests rather than those of the country concerned. The Americans were worried that a weak Eritrea might be vulnerable to a Communist takeover, leaving them in a dominant position at the vital entrance to the Red Sea. It was in America's interests that Eritrea be linked with their ally,

Ethiopia. In December 1952, the UN declared Eritrea an autonomous state federated with Ethiopia.

Haile Selassie immediately began to undermine the federation arrangements. Eritrean political parties were banned; Ethiopia appropriated Eritrea's shares of customs and excise; Eritrean newspapers were censored; in 1956, Tigrinya and Arabic were banned as teaching languages and replaced with Amharic; Eritrean industries were dismantled and relocated in Addis Ababa. In 1962, while the UN and the western powers discreetly looked the other way, Ethiopia illegally dissolved the federation and annexed Eritrea, declaring it the fourteenth province of Ethiopia.

The Eritrean fightback had begun in September 1961, when a group of eleven men under the leadership of Idris Hamid Awate formed the first contingent of the Eritrean Liberation Front (ELF) engaged in armed struggle against the ruling power. Within six months the movement had grown to a force of 500 who were harassing Ethiopian soldiers around Agordat, an important town in the centre of Eritrea. In December 1962 a group of policemen in Massawa, on the Eritrean coast, deserted to the ELF, taking with them arms and ammunition.

The Ethiopian regime reacted to the growing resistance with brutal force. Attacks against Ethiopian troops were countered with reprisals, often targeting the civilian population. Hundreds of civilians were massacred and whole villages burned. By the late 1960s thousands of refugees were fleeing across the border to Sudan. After the *Dergue* took over they had continued forcibly to resist Eritrean calls for independence.

My Eritrean friends told me that there were two factions within the independence movement, the ELF, and the Eritrean Peoples' Liberation Front (EPLF). As well as fighting the Ethiopians, they were fighting each other. The stronger faction, the EPLF, used to go from village to village recruiting fighters, including women, and ordering people to stop performing many of their traditional practices. If they didn't comply, the EPLF sometimes burned the villages. Most of the refugees in the camp were ELF supporters from western Eritrea who had fled. They were from a tribe called the Bin Amar. While the EPLF were Christian, the ELF were mostly Muslims.

The clinic workers were all EPLF. I was completely illiterate as far as politics were concerned. It just didn't register with me that as well as being persecuted by Ethiopia, great injustices were happening within Eritrea itself. I suppose I was too swept up by the grand dream of independence to analyse things too closely. Night after night, I listened to my friends passionately describing how they were going to build a free Eritrea. A new self-reliant, politically united nation was about to be born. It was heady stuff. I was captivated by it, and the rest of the western world would soon follow.

One of my friends, Kiros, who was a dresser, spoke a little English. On a few occasions he introduced me to cadres who had come over from Eritrea to visit him. I realise now he had probably informed them that there was an English-speaking white woman in the camp who was sympathetic to the cause. These cadres talked to me about their struggle and told me that I could be doing more than just working in a clinic, I could be helping them politically. In October 1977 I was thrilled to receive an invitation from the EPLF to visit Eritrea. They warned that it could be dangerous, but I hardly heard them. This was a chance to see history in the making. I didn't hesitate to say yes.

CHAPTER 4

In November I took a month's leave. Following instructions relayed to me via Kiros, I travelled to Port Sudan. The Sudanese government was very much opposed to the *Dergue* and had allowed the EPLF to set up a compound in a section of the port. It was a big complex, housing hundreds of people. There was a warehouse where food and weapons were stored; in a workshop, mechanics worked on tanks and military vehicles captured from the Ethiopians. The EPLF administration operated out of a building with a long verandah giving onto offices.

I was introduced to Isaias Afeworke, second-in-charge of the EPLF, who was later to become President of Eritrea. Like everyone else, he was dressed in khaki and wearing plastic sandals. He was clearly a leader. He was suave and, while everyone else's wrinkled in the heat, his clothes were always immaculately pressed. As we shook hands I got a whiff of cologne. Our first meeting took place in his office. He ushered me into a comfortable armchair and welcomed me in good English. He thanked me for showing interest in Eritrea. We talked for a little while about the situation inside the country. Despite the fact that they were fighting a guerilla war against tanks and artillery and jet fighter-bombers, he was absolutely confident of victory.

I also met the Chairman of the EPLF, Rammadan Mohammed Noor. I enjoyed his company much more than that of Afeworke. We had to converse in Arabic, which in my case was far from fluent. He was a lovely, conciliatory man, rather like a father. He loved to talk and joke. There was less of the fanatic about him than there was with Afeworke.

I was given a place to sleep in one of the EPLF houses. The officer who was assigned to look after me suggested that I undergo weapons training. I told him no thanks, I would be hopeless at handling a gun.

'You could learn,' he said. 'We have women who are fighting.'

When I refused again, he shrugged his shoulders in acceptance.

We set off in a convoy of half a dozen trucks filled with food, weapons, and young soldiers going to fight. They were just boys, many of them merely teenagers. The oldest would have been in his early twenties. They were fired up with patriotism, singing revolutionary songs as we rolled along.

We followed the coast south-east to Suakin, an old Turkish fort, then in broad daylight crossed the border into Eritrea. Once inside Eritrea, we turned south into semi-desert country. The atmosphere in my truck noticeably changed. Before, the soldiers had been full of bravado; now, they were quiet and on edge. Their tenseness rubbed off on me. From now on we would be exposed to attack from MiG jet fighters that the Russians were supplying to their Communist comrades, the *Dergue*. As if to remind us of the danger, now and then we came across burnt-out vehicles which had been destroyed in air attacks.

A couple of times our camouflaged vehicles halted and the engines were switched off. In the distance we heard the faint sound of jet engines. Fortunately, the MiGs were too far away to sight us and we couldn't see them. At night we travelled without lights.

On the second day we were caught in a tremendous wind storm. The air was thick with choking yellow sand. The convoy came to a halt, as it was impossible to see more than a couple of metres ahead. For four or five hours we huddled in the trucks with scarves around our faces, barely able to breathe. The sand crept under my clothing, into my ears and nose and every fold of skin. My hair was caked with the stuff. When the wind finally died down I rose stiffly to my feet and a bucketful cascaded from my clothes onto the ground.

During the next three weeks I visited several towns in areas which had been liberated from Ethiopia. I saw for the first time what I had been hearing about for so long. This was a war of brutal military power against unquenchable spirit. Whenever the Eritreans tried to farm their land the MiGs would come down out of the sky to strafe and bomb them. As a result, people all over the country were starving. Their strategy in this mismatched contest was to go underground. They lived in caves and in tunnels dug into mountains. Underground factories manufactured everything from shoes to sanitary pads. Schools, military command posts, even hospitals with operating theatres, were all underground. The hospitals were spotlessly clean and the doctors were as skilled as any I'd seen.

Everywhere I went I came across young men and women who were disfigured, blinded, crippled, missing limbs. Yet their spirit remained strong. Much of the country had been liberated. The capital, Asmara, remained under Ethiopian occupation but the Eritreans were convinced that victory was coming very soon.

Towards the end of my trip my guides took me to the front line close to Asmara. Here was fighting as it must have been in the First World War. The opposing sides were lined up facing one another in trenches. Every now and then they'd let loose an artillery barrage, or they'd sneak a couple of rifle shots, aiming with a periscope over the top of the parapet.

Stupidly, I put my head up to take a quick look at the other side. There was a sharp crack and a bullet literally parted my hair. I hit the dirt shaking. The soldiers fell about laughing, then scolded me for being so careless, as we all had to lie on the ground for a while until it was deemed safe to move.

I hadn't told my family that I was going to Eritrea because I knew they'd be worried. When I came back to Sudan, I wrote a letter to my parents telling them all about it. I mentioned also that I'd been learning to speak Tigrinya. Mother wrote back in her usual supportive way. And, as usual, Father scribbled a few words at the bottom. He wrote that it was nice that I'd been to Eritrea but, if I really wanted to know all about the country, I should visit the British Museum. 'And I'm so glad you've learned to speak Swahili,' he added.

I was full of excitement about what I'd seen. I was determined to do what I could to further the Eritrean cause. Of course, that was exactly what the EPLF had intended.

My work at the clinic was as demanding as ever. I knew from my forays into the camp that there was a vast number of sick people whom I never saw. Some visits to people's homes were heart-breaking. In one particularly poor part of the camp, practically everyone had lost family members. Many were so ill that they couldn't get out of bed. The frustrating thing was that they sometimes lay there for months because it simply did not occur to them to ask for help. One especially upsetting case was that of a young girl without parents, who had TB in her spine. When I found her, she had been bed-ridden for six months. I saw her often, as it took about 60 injections to cure her.

The EPLF had obviously noted my enthusiasm for their

cause. In about mid-1978, I received another delegation from across the border. The western media had suddenly discovered their struggle and increasing numbers of journalists wanted to see the war for themselves. The delegation asked if I would be prepared to go in again, this time helping to look after the media.

A week or so later I was once again in the EPLF compound in Port Sudan. One night there was an informal gathering of EPLF officers in Afeworke's office. A long and involved argument developed over the merits of different forms of social-ism. At that time the big three were Maoism, Albanian Socialism, and pure Marxism. Afeworke favoured the so-called 'Gang of Four' version of Maoism. Some of his people were arguing that none of them was suitable for Eritrea, that they should develop their own political system. Afeworke told them, 'You follow me or nothing.' They talked on and on for hours, becoming quite heated. A few people left. I thought it was a ridiculous argument and, after a while, went to bed. In the hours before dawn I heard two gun shots. I knew Afeworke kept a little polished pistol in his drawer, as I'd seen it.

I didn't know what to think. It shows how blinded I was by idealism that even hearing gun shots did not give me pause. Later that same day I was once again in a rattling truck heading for the border, this time with people from the *Washington Post*, the BBC, Swedish Television and other media organisations.

We had an EPLF guide with us who organised everything. I can't remember his name, but I will certainly never forget what he looked like because of a bad experience I had a few years later. I'll tell that story a little further on. My job was to keep these hardened journalists happy, especially when they had to wait for things to happen. The EPLF gave me some bottles of liquor and a pack of playing cards. Being completely ignorant about alcohol, I asked what I was supposed to do with the booze. Did I mix one with the other or what, exactly?

'Don't worry,' they said, 'they're journalists. They'll know what to do.'

On the whole, I got on pretty well with the gentlemen (they were all men) of the press. The only time they became difficult was when I had to keep them waiting to go to the front. When I asked the guide how I was supposed to entertain them, he suggested I tell some English jokes. The trouble was that I didn't know any. The journalists all had deadlines to meet and they didn't take kindly to being chaperoned.

We spent a lot of time in and around the front lines. I did a lot of walking. One day the guide took me on foot to within 4 kilometres of Asmara, which was still in Ethiopian hands.

From the EPLF's point of view, the trip was a big success. The journalists all went away and wrote favourable reports about this tiny nation struggling valiantly against a brutal aggressor. It was the beginning of the western world's love affair with Eritrea.

Back home in Australia Rowene was also working for the cause, thanks to her friendship with the four boys we had sponsored, and to the arrival, in April 1978, of another young Eritrean, Fessahaie Abraham. I'd met Fessahaie in Sudan just after I'd returned from my first visit to Eritrea. He had come to see me in the camp with quite a story. He and one of Tadesse's friends had worked for SIM in Addis Ababa. Inspired by Tadesse's success at getting into Australia, Fessahaie had decided to try it himself. His efforts had taken him on a tortuous journey to a refugee camp in Somalia, then to prison in Kenya, where he was held as an illegal immigrant. After seven months' incarceration, he had been released and allowed to go to Sudan. During this time, he had been writing to people in Australia trying to obtain student sponsorship. One of them was Rowene, who had been doing her best for him. When I met him the University of New South Wales had accepted him as a student but he still had many hurdles to jump before the Australian government would allow him in. Fessahaie wanted to know if I could do anything to help.

I said I would help if I could, but before I could really begin, the United Nations High Commission for Refugees in Khartoum took up his case and he was at last given permission to go to Australia.

Fessahaie didn't have a bean to his name so I paid for his airfare. Rowene met him in Sydney. Along with Tadesse and the other Eritrean boys, they had set up the Eritrean Relief Association.

The other big thing in Rowene's life was that she had married an engineer, Harvey Dillon, who was involved with hearing aid research. In late 1978, they came to Khartoum for a visit. Although I hadn't seen her for two years, our friendship picked up right where we had left it.

Rowene told me that I had changed a lot. I suppose two years living pretty much like a refugee myself must have made some difference. Speaking Arabic and Tigrinya all the time had apparently affected my English: Rowene reckoned that I had a strange accent and I put the inflections in the wrong places. In fact, I'm aware that my English is still a little strange.

Rowene and I talked nonstop. She confided that, despite being married, she was still finding it hard to settle down in Australia. We were both passionate about Eritrea. It's not too strong a description to say that we were obsessed.

*

I had originally intended working at Wad el Hilaywa for six months. This had stretched to more than two years. I was happy to keep going but the EPLF asked me to go back to Australia to help with the establishment of the Eritrean Relief Association, and I agreed. As well as becoming involved with the Eritrean struggle, I had been hearing a lot about what was going on in Ethiopia. It sounded like Stalinist Russia. The military leader, Major Mengistu, had closed the universities and sent the students into the countryside to help 're-educate' the peasants. Their smallholdings were all being incorporated into big collective farms modelled on those in the Soviet Union. Businesses had been nationalised, middle-class people were labelled 'bourgeois' and had their homes confiscated. A vast network of spies informed against anyone who dared to speak out against the *Dergue*. In 1978, in the notorious 'Red Terror Campaign', the regime had killed hundreds of 'intellectuals', mainly university students since their intellect was considered a danger to developing socialism. I'd heard that a number of people I'd known in my first visit had been killed or imprisoned, and that many Ethiopian and Christian leaders had been murdered in the south of the country and their families left in hardship. Because of the regime's iron control, the situation was barely reported in the outside world.

These stories stirred my sense of injustice. In Eritrea I had seen how influential the news media could be. I thought that if I could only get into Ethiopia, I might be able to investigate the situation and alert people to what was going on. Kirsty Wright, the Asme-Humanitas representative, knew the Ethiopian ambassador in Khartoum. In January 1979 she took me to see him. He said that visiting Ethiopia was not possible at the moment. I asked if that was because there was some trouble in the country. He denied it. I told him that all I wanted to do was visit old friends at the mission where I'd worked, since I was going back to Australia. He repeated that, for the time being, there could be no foreign visitors.

A few days later Kirsty told me that the ambassador had gone on a visit to Kenya; she suggested I try his secretary. I gave him a story that the ambassador had agreed to my going but, in all the discussion, he had forgotten to stamp my passport. The secretary obliged, and that same night I took a flight to Addis Ababa.

The capital looked very different from when I had last seen it four years earlier. There were big pictures of Mengistu everywhere; red banners with socialist slogans decorated many of the buildings. The main roads all had military checkpoints. I made contact with some young people whom I had known before and they agreed to help me gather information. I was distressed to hear that some of my friends from Alamata had been among those killed by the *Dergue*.

We moved around mostly at night, taking care to avoid the checkpoints. Often we could hear gunfire as the *Dergue* soldiers went about their grim business of suppression. My young guides showed me where people had been killed, or abducted, never to be seen again. I met people who had been imprisoned and tortured so badly that they couldn't walk. They gave me the names of men, women and children who had been tortured and killed, sometimes on the say-so of informants who may have had purely personal motives for betraying them. I carefully noted down all the names and details.

Among the few missions left was my old employer, the SIM. I called on my former bosses to ask about reports of missionaries in the south being imprisoned. They told me they hadn't been imprisoned, they'd been killed.

I asked about reports of their families being ostracised and no one being allowed to help them or feed them.

They confirmed that this was the case. 'Praise be to God,' one added.

I said, 'What? Praise be to God because people are suffering? What sort of mission is this?'

'You should know your Bible. The church must be prepared to endure pain and suffering.'

'I know I'm young and you're old,' I replied, 'but what I think is this: we're international people, we have easygoing governments and free speech. Why don't we talk about these people's problems so the whole world hears about it, and maybe we can stop it? People will say, "How dare you? Why forbid these wives and children from getting food because their husband or father is a pastor?" It's not fair that they should have to suffer in such terrible circumstances.'

They remonstrated: 'You don't understand. We remember when you were here before. You always get the wrong end of the story. You're not very Christian in your outlook.'

I shook my head, incredulous. 'I'm very sad when I hear that people I used to know have died; these young boys I worked with in Alamata. I think this is awful. I also heard from the local people that a whole truckload of children's bodies was dumped outside your compound. What did you do about that?'

'We did nothing. If we spoke up we would have been thrown out of the country. It's better to stay; therefore, we kept quiet.'

'What? These are children, the world cries for children. How could you do this? You're supposed to be godly people.'

'This is the will of God.'

I was very upset. I told them that when I left Ethiopia, I was going to tell everyone what was going on.

'Don't you dare do that, you'll only stir up more trouble.'

'Leave it to me. Just leave it to me.'

I was in Addis for five days – five days of constant anxiety. I knew that if the *Dergue* caught me, I'd be killed. On the day

I left I was trembling as I approached the immigration counter. The officer peered at my passport, looked at me, back to the passport, then at me again. I stood absolutely still, hoping that he could not sense my fear. Not a word was said. Eventually, after about a year, he stamped the passport and waved me through. It was another eternity before the boarding announcement came. Only when the plane took off and I saw the land drop away, did I begin to relax.

My destination was London. As soon as I arrived, I called the BBC and told them what I'd been doing.

'Lovely,' they said. 'We'd like to interview you.'

The interview went out on the World Service in the *Focus on Africa* program. The BBC received many phone calls afterwards, including one from a woman missionary in Sweden who had recently been expelled. She thanked me for telling the truth. She had been too afraid to speak out.

After the BBC broadcast I gave my report to Amnesty International. And then, suddenly, there was nothing to do. London in the middle of winter was an alien place. I hated the crowded trains, the pinched white faces of people hurrying everywhere, the cold and the rain. The warmth and space and friendliness of Australia beckoned. It was time to go back, at least for a while.

CHAPTER 5

In Sydney, I got a job straightaway doing neonatal nursing at Randwick Children's Hospital. I worked in the intensive care department looking after tiny premature babies, some weighing as little as 800 grams. I loved the work, and I enjoyed the luxury of a well-equipped hospital with proper ethical standards. I especially appreciated not having to brush flies away all the time.

I was sleeping one day after a stint of night duty when the telephone woke me. It was someone from the Department of Foreign Affairs in Canberra. He informed me that the Ethiopian government had declared me *persona non grata*. 'If you ever travel there again, you can expect the worst,' he warned. 'The Australian government will not be responsible. Your passport cannot help you.'

It was the first time I had received a warning like that, but it would not be the last.

Fessahaie had arrived in Sydney too late to begin his university course. He had to wait a whole year until the next intake. In the meantime, he had taken a job working night shift in a factory. During the day, he and Rowene had been making phone calls and writing letters asking for help for Eritrea.

I had been writing similar letters from Sudan; one had been to the Australian Council of Churches (ACC). The head of their overseas aid section, Martin Chittleborough, no doubt received many requests from people seeking assistance for various causes. Seeing my name at the bottom of the letter, he remarked to a colleague, 'There's a priest named Browning in the Newcastle diocese. I wonder if he's related?'

When he rang my brother, George put in a good word for me. So that was a promising start. At about the same time, Fessahaie and Rowene had come to the ACC also seeking assistance. The link between us was discovered and the upshot was that the ACC had agreed to help set up the Eritrean Relief Association (ERA). They gave Fessahaie and Rowene a desk and a telephone in the Sydney office, and offered to help with administration.

By the time I arrived home, the ERA was up and running. I couldn't wait to pitch in. I arranged my shifts so that I was working at night as much as possible. I'd have a few hours' sleep in the morning, then spend the rest of the day telephoning and writing letters to the news media, parliamentarians, church and community leaders, aid agencies – anyone whom I thought might help. When I could find the time, I spoke to church and community groups.

The world was by now quite enamoured of this obscure war in the Horn of Africa. The *Women's Weekly* did a big spread on Eritrea. I was interviewed on radio and TV and was quoted in newspaper articles. As a result, I was recognised in the street once or twice. One morning, travelling on the bus from Bondi into the city, a passenger did a double take and said, 'Hello, Eritrea, how are you today?'

The ACC had given us a seeding grant of $450. Before the end of that first year, we had made our first big breakthrough. A combination of aid agencies, including AusAID, Australian Catholic Relief, Community Aid Abroad and the Freedom from

Hunger Campaign, contributed $80,000. From then on, things moved quickly; the amounts being donated grew into the hundreds of thousands of dollars.

There were still frustrations, however. One obstacle was that the Australian government only gave aid on a government-to-government basis. Even though the ERA was a registered humanitarian organisation, the government wouldn't deal with us because of our links with the EPLF. I made a few visits to Canberra with Fessahaie to lobby MPs. At a meeting with the Minister for Foreign Affairs, Andrew Peacock, we argued that it was quite feasible for the government to land aid at the port of Massawa, which was under Eritrean control. The government was worried about security, they were worried about whether the ERA had the capacity to distribute it – they were worried about a lot of things. There were always reasons why it couldn't be done.

In 1982, the Senate Committee on Foreign Affairs and Trade held an enquiry into the whole issue of how they should be providing aid to areas of conflict, in particular the Horn of Africa. I gave a presentation arguing that if you only work through governments, you automatically exclude a large group of people within a conflict zone. The Ethiopians, for example, certainly weren't going to distribute aid to Eritrea, even though they claimed it as a province, because it would only help the very people they were fighting.

After many days of hearings the committee came up with a finding that changed the whole nature of government aid. They recommended that, in future, aid could be given to people who were within rebel-held areas, provided it was done at arm's length through a non-government organisation. This opened the way for staunch supporters such as the Australian Council of Churches to approach the government directly for food aid. It began as a trickle. By 1983, the amount of aid from Australia to Eritrea totalled about $6 million a year.

*

The Eritreans were not the only liberation movement struggling for a voice in the region. The Tigray People's Liberation Front (TPLF), representing the province of Tigray next to the Eritrean border, was fighting a bitter war with Ethiopia, as were Somalis in Ethiopia, under the banner of the Ogaden National Liberation Front. The Oromo Liberation Front represented the Oromo people in Ethiopia. The Afar had the Afar Liberation Front. And there was also the Ethiopian People's Revolutionary Party, largely comprising intellectual Amharas. Even some of Haile Selassie's family members had a liberation front. Exiled members of these groups used to meet in the tea shops of Khartoum, arguing and plotting and dreaming of the day when they would achieve glorious victory in the lands they claimed as their own.

Back in Australia, I had a glorious dream of my own. With the success of the ERA, I had been taking more and more interest in these other causes. I thought that if only we could get them all to come together, they could help one another and be more effective. Also, it would help Australia to focus more on the region. I formed an organisation called The Horn of Africa Committee. I knew the Eritreans would never get involved, but the Ogadens did, and the Oromos. Some Amharas were in, but not all. The Tigray people were nearly in but not quite. When I think of it now, it was an impossible idea, trying to get these diverse groups with their different agendas to work together. For all the time I'd spent in the region, I was still a political novice; or perhaps I was just too idealistic for my own good.

I was still involved with the Eritreans. In about 1980, I think it was, I can't remember exactly, I had made a fact-finding trip back to Sudan. When I returned to Australia, I spoke to the media not only about Eritrea but about these other liberation movements.

Shortly afterwards I received word that Isaias Afeworke was

displeased. He warned me that I was to speak only about Eritrean matters. I've never taken kindly to people telling me what to do, so, naturally, I just went right on the way I was going. A year or so later I made another trip to the Horn, and went to the EPLF compound in Port Sudan. I had a face-to-face meeting with Afeworke. He was furious. 'I warned you to speak only about the EPLF,' he thundered. 'You have disobeyed me.'

I told him I'd speak about what I liked – the EPLF didn't own me. That's when he threatened me. 'You will see what I will do,' he said.

'You'll do nothing. I have an Australian passport. I'm not Eritrean, I'm Australian.'

'You belong to us,' he said. 'We created you.'

'I do not belong to you. I can call upon the Australian government to assist me. So, don't you threaten me.'

When I arrived home, Afeworke had already put the word out. None of my Eritrean friends would have anything to do with me. After such an optimistic beginning, it was a disappointing way to end my involvement with Eritrea.

In the meantime, Fessahaie had enrolled at the University of New South Wales as a chemical engineering student. He still continued his work with the ERA. One day he went to consult the eye surgeon, Professor Fred Hollows, about trouble he was having with his vision. As well as being a noted surgeon, and teaching at the university, Hollows was blessed with more than the usual share of compassion for his fellow man. He was well known for his trips into the Australian outback, where he was restoring sight to Aboriginal people blinded by trachoma. When Fessahaie told him about the revolution that was taking place in Eritrea, Hollows, like so many others, was immediately enthused. With Fessahaie's help, he would eventually perform his operations in Eritrea, and set up a factory for the manufacture of intraocular lenses to replace lenses which had been destroyed by cataracts.

Hollows was not the only celebrated Australian to fall under Eritrea's spell. In 1989, the author Thomas Keneally travelled the by now well-worn route into the ravaged country. His novel *Towards Asmara* gave a rose-coloured account of the struggle for independence.

By the end of the 1980s, the TPLF and the EPLF had formed an alliance against their mutual enemy. At the same time, Ethiopia suffered a major blow when the Soviet Union withdrew its support. The Eritrean forces rallied, recapturing many towns which had been in Ethiopian hands. The morale of the Ethiopian troops was in tatters. The regime began to totter. In 1988, the EPLF captured Afabet, the headquarters of the Ethiopian army in north-eastern Eritrea. The following year, they captured once more the strategic port town of Massawa, and, in 1991, they liberated the capital, Asmara.

In that same year, a combined force of the TPLF and the EPLF swept south, pushing the Ethiopian army before them. Just before they marched into Addis Ababa, Mengistu escaped in a private aircraft to Zimbabwe. There, his pal the president, Robert Mugabe, gave him sanctuary. Two years later, in 1993, a referendum in Eritrea voted unanimously to become an independent republic. The victory had been achieved at a crippling cost. It's estimated that 60,000 Eritreans died in the war, 50,000 children lost their parents and 60,000 people were left maimed.

The new president was Isaias Afeworke. The leader of the TPLF, Meles Zenawi, became the President of Ethiopia. The two men are cousins, which you'd think would augur well for future relations. In October 1993, Fessahaie was appointed the first Eritrean ambassador to Australia.

So, a happy ending to the story, you think? Unfortunately, in

Africa things are rarely so simple. In 1998, war broke out once more, ending two years later with an uneasy ceasefire agreement. As I write, seven years after the ceasefire, the two nations remain bitter enemies. The two armies are facing off again over a disputed section of border; occasional skirmishes are still occurring. A society which should be united is divided, and the fear never leaves that war will one day break out again.

The grand vision of an ideal society, which seduced us all, has turned to ashes. Far from being a country where there is equality for everyone, Eritrea has turned into a dictatorship where people who speak out against the regime may disappear or be thrown into prison for years without trial. Because of its poor human rights record, Eritrea is shunned by most democratic countries. Increasingly, it is turning its attention to other isolated groups. Eritrea is supplying arms and troops to the opposition Islamic Council in Somalia, while Ethiopia backs the interim government on behalf of the USA. The strategy seems to be to stretch Ethiopian resources thin by opening up a second front. Its near neighbours, Sudan and Djibouti, are nervous about Eritrea's intentions. At home, Afeworke has imposed impossible conditions upon the international aid agencies he so sorely needs. He has banned them from development activities, telling them they can only do food aid; and the food must only be distributed by the government. He has forced them to exchange money at a special, exorbitant, rate; arbitrarily banned many foreign aid workers; and refused to account for the government's use of aid money. It has become so bad that almost all aid agencies have packed up and left, at a time when he needs them more than ever before. From 2001 to 2005, the country was stricken by drought, causing tremendous hardship amongst the rural peasant population. Eritrea is one of the poorest nations, with one of the worst human rights records, in Africa. With hindsight, I believe we probably did the wrong thing promoting

Eritrean independence. We'd have been better off trying to facilitate people of different cultures and religions living together in peace, regardless of borders.

Rowene's marriage to Harvey lasted for ten years before ending in divorce. Rowene says the main thing that came between them was her obsession with Eritrea. Considering how things turned out, I find it ironic that, in 1981, I was awarded the RSL peace prize for my activities in Africa.

But I should return to my story, where many of these outcomes were yet to take place. I had become more and more involved with refugees, especially Somalis. By 1984, I was keen to return to Africa, but this time I did not want to work in a refugee camp. For what I had in mind, I'd need a visa which would enable me to stay in Somalia for a long time. This was not possible in Australia but there was one place I knew I could get it – Saudi Arabia.

CHAPTER 6

The King Faisal Military Hospital had been built by the Americans in the late 1970s, at Khamis Mushayt, near Saudi Arabia's border with Yemen. It was well equipped, and included a burns unit, a male medical and surgical ward, paediatrics and obstetrics departments. The neonatal intensive care ward, where I worked, was an up-to-date facility with 30 beds.

Most of the medical staff were foreigners. Amongst the nurses, there were Australians, French, Americans and Britons and a large number of Filippinas. Most of us lived in nurses' quarters within the hospital compound.

I became friends with a fellow Australian, who was from Melbourne: Dianne 'Dottie' Bartram. Dottie was a forthright, cheerful lady who was always ready for a laugh. She had worked in Saudi before, between 1981 to 1983. When she'd returned home she'd found it impossible to settle, so she'd come back for another stint.

As I got to know Dottie, I found that her fun-loving persona complemented a thoughtful, caring nature. I was attracted to this serious side of her. I could talk to Dottie about anything –

the state of the world, refugee problems in Africa, my plans for the future . . . she would always listen.

A frequent subject of our conversations was the appalling plight of women in Saudi Arabia. They had absolutely no rights, being wholly the chattels of men. Women had to be completely covered when they went outside the house; they were not allowed to drive a car or travel with a man other than their husband or a close relative; if they rode alone in a bus, they had to sit at the back in a space reserved for females.

Saudi men held themselves up to be devout Muslims and men of prayer, yet, often when I was working the evening shift, we'd get a phone call from some man saying there was a car cruising outside the compound, a Mercedes or whatever, and he had a party to go to with plenty of booze. Amazingly, some of the girls actually took up these invitations, which was a very dangerous thing to do. Just before I'd arrived, two Filippina nurses had been raped and murdered, and I saw many instances of others having unpleasant experiences. Perhaps because I was a bit of a party pooper myself, the girls often came to me to get them out of trouble. It helped that I had learned to speak a bit of Arabic in Sudan.

One morning I'd just gone to bed after a night shift when some nurses came running to my room saying that someone was being attacked. I threw on some clothes over my pyjamas and hurried to the hospital post office. A few girls were standing anxiously in front of a car, preventing it from moving. Inside, was an Australian girl with a Saudi man. She'd gone to the post office to buy some stamps and leaned over the counter for a normal, friendly chat. This conceited oaf thought she was coming on to him. He'd locked the post office, forced her into the car, and was about to drive off when some of her friends saw what was happening.

I knew enough about Saudi men's notions of superiority to

know that he wouldn't take much notice of me. Instead, I spoke to the girl, putting on an angry voice and berating her for being in a car with a man. While I kept on talking, I was opening the door, saying to the driver, 'I'm so sorry this could have happened, this is just a rubbish girl.' Then, to the girl, 'How dare you bring shame upon us, get to your room.'

Luckily, the would-be assailant was confused enough by all the fuss for us to get away with it.

Saudi men had absolutely no idea how to act normally with women, even ones of their own nationality. Mothers who came to the hospital to have their babies often confided in me. I could speak Arabic, I was a foreigner and a nurse, and perhaps they were drawn to me for those reasons.

One woman whose daughter had just given birth to a premature baby was very upset. She said, 'I'm 35, no older than you, and I'm a grandmother. My husband has just married a second wife who's a friend of my daughter. I'm so humiliated, I don't know what to do. She's around the house all the time and I feel as if I'm nobody.' She pleaded with me to take her away to Australia. I had to tell her that was impossible.

A new father once told me how pleased he was that he'd had a girl because she would be cheaper than a boy. He wouldn't have to educate her, just marry her off.

I asked him, 'Why don't girls need an education?'

'They don't have such a high intellect,' he said. 'Don't you know that? They haven't got the ability to reason or calculate. That's why we have wives as servants. '

'I didn't know that. Who tells you that?'

'It's in the Koran.'

I said, 'Where in the Koran? I have an English version, shall I bring it out?'

He quickly changed the subject.

*

One day a woman arrived screaming hysterically. They couldn't find the usual translator, so they called me down from the neonatal ward. I asked her what the problem was.

She said, 'I need help, I'm bleeding and the bleeding isn't normal.'

'What do you mean?'

'I've cut myself.'

'Cut yourself where?' I couldn't see any sign of bleeding.

She pointed to her lower abdomen hidden beneath voluminous robes. I thought perhaps she had had a miscarriage. I hurried her into a consulting room and closed the door. She lifted her garments and, sobbing uncontrollably, explained to me that she had stuck a knife into her vagina and cut herself open.

'You've made a mess of yourself, my dear. Why have you done this?'

'Because I wanted the doctor to tell my husband he mustn't touch me for a week. He never leaves me alone. I get no sleep, I'm a slave for him day and night. I'm never at rest. I don't know what to do with myself.'

I'd seen some disturbing things in refugee camps but never anything like this. I could scarcely imagine the utter despair which must have driven her to this. With the help of a couple of nurses, I repaired her injury. I then went to the doctor in charge of emergency and described to him what had happened. I told him that we had stopped the bleeding and stitched the cut, high in the vagina, but that the patient wanted a male doctor to speak to her husband.

The doctor, a sympathetic British man, agreed. 'You translate what I say and I'll tell him she's very seriously ill and if he touches her, he'll get the sickness. He's not to touch her for a month.'

I explained all this to the husband, a thin, worried-looking man with, typically, a couple of days' growth of beard. He listened meekly and agreed to do as we asked.

I then told his wife what we'd said. 'He agrees not to touch you for a month.'

'A month?' She leapt off the bed and started kissing me. 'Which doctor, which doctor?'

I pointed out the doctor, and she went over and kissed *him*. 'Thank you, oh, thank you. This is the best day of my life. A month. It's too wonderful.'

She was in her late twenties; a typical Saudi wife. Her role in life to cater to the whims of men.

There was a lively social scene at the hospital, if you were interested. There was a swimming pool, but men and women weren't allowed to use it at the same time. Dottie used to take tennis lessons when she first arrived, but the hospital management put a stop to that when they realised that the coach was a male. There were lots of parties thrown by other expatriates, who also often went away for weekends camping beside the Red Sea. I preferred to spend my time with one or two locals outside the hospital, with whom I had made friends.

Zahara was a Somali woman whose brother I had known in Australia. When I went to visit her in her house in Khamis Mushayt, we hit it off immediately. She was a small woman with beautiful black skin and fine Somali features. She had six children and had recently been divorced from her husband, who was a businessman.

I spent many of my days off with Zahara, playing with the children, shopping, cooking, watching TV, talking and talking. I liked her very much. She was strong-minded and funny; we laughed at the same things.

One day someone I didn't know rang from Zahara's house and told me that something terrible had happened. I rushed over. A police officer opened the door. Zahara, he said, was dead.

Somehow, some Saudi men had tricked her into getting into a car with them. They'd driven her up into the mountains along a winding, precipitous road. She knew what was going to happen. As they had rounded a bend, she had opened the door and thrown herself out, falling to her death.

Dear Zahara. Because she was a divorcée and a foreigner, she was fair game.

One of the good things to come out of my time in Saudi Arabia was my friendship with Dottie. That continues to this day. Dottie is now in Melbourne and, although I live on the other side of the world, she and Rowene are my dearest friends.

On the whole, though, I can't say that I greatly enjoyed my year in Saudi Arabia. I was disgusted by the hypocrisy I saw and the abuses of human rights. But I was there for one reason only, as a stepping stone to Somalia. At the end of the year, I went to see the Somalian ambassador in Riyadh. He couldn't have been more obliging, offering to give me a passport if I wished! I told him that a decent visa would be fine, thank you. He obliged with a permanent re-entry visa, which meant that I could go in and out of Somalia as often and for as long as I wished.

CHAPTER 7

Somalia was being swamped with refugees fleeing from neighbouring Ethiopia. It had been eleven years since Mengistu had taken over the country by force and murdered Emperor Haile Selassie. During that time, Ethiopia had descended further and further into chaos. The refugees included peasants fleeing 'villagisation', by which small farmers were being resettled into villages while their lands were lumped together into state-run collectives. Many preferred to flee the country rather than submit to the Communist system. Others, from different ethnic groups, such as Tigrayans, Oromos and Amharas, were engaged in wars of liberation with the central government.

It was 1985. Since the previous year, Ethiopia had been ravaged by another famine as devastating as the one with which Rowene and I had been involved in 1974. Hundreds of thousands of people had died. There were rumours that aid destined for famine victims had been diverted to the military, who were still engaged in the interminable war with Eritrea. If this was true, it was a shocking crime. My chief reason for going to Somalia was to gather evidence through interviewing refugees. I planned to take it to the contacts I'd made at the BBC and to Amnesty International.

I was well aware that it was dangerous for a woman to travel alone in Somalia. Whilst not as bad as Saudis, Somali men nevertheless had an unsavoury reputation. I had to keep my wits about me all the time. I usually travelled on buses and trucks, only accepting a lift in a car if there were other women in it. I was careful not to get myself into tricky situations. It saddened me that I had to be this way, because it's my nature to be friendly and open with everyone I meet.

I visited refugee camps all over the country. And what camps they were! One, outside Hargeysa, run by World Vision, held 120,000 people living in a vast city of tents. There were half a dozen others of similar size dotted around the country. In all, there were over 700,000 refugees in Somalia, one of the biggest refugee inflows in history.

My possessions consisted of a pair of jeans, a couple of shirts and a T-shirt or two. I carried these, and a few other bits and pieces, in a small bag which I slung over my shoulder. I didn't care much where I slept – still don't, if it comes to that – if someone was generous enough to offer me a bed or a corner of a clinic in one of the camps, that would do me.

The one place I was guaranteed a bed was in the capital, Mogadishu, where I had to return now and then to send my reports to the BBC's African Service. I stayed with the family of a Somali boy I'd known in Australia. It was a typical Somali household, with three generations all living together under the one roof. The patriarch was a retired army man. His oldest son, Mohammad, the brother of my friend in Australia, was also in the army and they had five children. They were very kind to me. As a friend of the family, their house was my house.

I had my own room. One evening, I was lying in bed in the dark, on the verge of sleep. A long pole came snaking in through the open window. In my half-awake state, I thought to myself, is this a dream? Perhaps I'm about to get malaria and I've got a fever.

I continued to watch in a detached way as the pole cautiously approached my clothes on a hanger on the wall, then deftly lifted them up. It was only when they disappeared out the window, that I realised this wasn't some fevered dream.

I sat up in a hurry and shouted at the top of my voice. Mohammad came running and we rushed out into the lane which ran along the back of the house. Too late. The thief had taken practically all the clothes I owned. I had to borrow some from Mohammad's wife and his teenage daughter until I replaced them.

The BBC was happy with my work. I filed many stories about the refugee situation within Somalia, reporting on whether the food levels were enough, how the distribution was working and so on. I was hoping to keep the attention of the west focused on Somalia, as I knew how quickly people move on. I was also attempting to paint an accurate picture of life in Ethiopia as told to me by refugees. The Ethiopians countered my reports with their own propaganda, insisting that everything was just beautiful in the Communist paradise.

The preferred way to file my reports was by telephone. Often, the overseas connections didn't work. Then I had to go and stand in line at Somalia's one telegraph office and send it in printed form, which someone would then read out on the radio. After a while I became so well known that the officials used to usher me straight to the front of the queue.

I got to know the BBC people in London quite well. After I'd phoned in one report, my contact asked, 'Are you receiving payments from us?'

Payments? It hadn't occurred to me that I could be paid for

what I was doing. I'd been living on the salary I'd saved from Saudi Arabia. When the BBC man had got over his surprise, he took down my banking details. From then on, whenever I sent a report a cheque would follow.

I'd been in Somalia for about a year when I went north to the border between Ethiopia and Somaliland for a routine visit. At the checkpoint at Hargeysa, I counted 800 people crossing over in one day, a fact I duly mentioned in a report to the BBC. A day after the broadcast, the Ethiopian government put out a statement accusing me of lying. It was not true that people were fleeing, they said. Why would they? Ethiopians lived in a Communist heaven.

It was a routine denial of a routine report, nothing that hadn't happened many times in the past. This time, though, the repercussions turned serious. Soldiers acting on the orders of the military governor of Somaliland, General Morgan, came to the hotel where I was staying and demanded that I accompany them to a meeting with their boss.

General Morgan told me that questions had been raised about my estimate of the number of refugees.

I told him I knew there had been 800. I'd counted them personally.

The general had a reputation for being a bully, and now I saw it firsthand. 'Not good enough,' he said, more aggressively than he needed to. 'You have to substantiate your figures from other sources.'

'The only other sources are in Ethiopia.'

'Well, if you don't substantiate it,' said the general, 'I'm going to throw you out.'

'Fine.' I replied, 'Throw me out. I'm here as a volunteer. I'm spending my money, not yours. All I'm doing is trying to raise more money for the refugees so they won't be such a burden on your country. If you throw me out, I'll just go to Australia.'

Like me, the general wanted more assistance for the refugees. He thought that if I could verify my reports from other sources, the Ethiopian regime would be unable to dispute them. It showed a lack of understanding of the way totalitarian regimes work. It wouldn't have mattered how much verification I had, they still would have denied there was a problem.

I'd been sending copies of all my stories to the United Nations High Commission for Refugees (UNHCR) in Mogadishu. I'd built up a good relationship with the man in charge. I asked him for his advice. 'You should go into Ethiopia,' he said. 'Get the story substantiated from that side.'

I asked him how he thought I could go to Ethiopia, which was being run like a police state.

He told me it would be easy. I should go to Djibouti, the port city in the independent nation of the same name, at the entrance to the Red Sea. A railway goes south-west from there into Ethiopia and all the way to Addis Ababa. He suggested I could cross the border by train and get off at Dire Dawa, which was in the area where the refugees were coming from. I could visit the villages and gather my evidence there.

I didn't like to tell him that I'd been declared *persona non grata*. But that had been many years ago; maybe the Ethiopians had forgotten about it by now. He said that his counterpart in the UNHCR office in Djibouti would surely be pleased to help me. He gave me his name and promised to let him know I was coming. I should have asked the UNHCR man in Mogadishu for a letter of introduction, but I didn't. That proved to be a significant mistake.

I'd never been to Djibouti. The day I left Somaliland, I was feeling distinctly unwell. And, as the flight went on, I became worse. I thought I must have had a burst ovary or something, the pain in my insides was so bad. I spent the flight doubled over, sweating and fighting off nausea.

When we landed, the officer at immigration took one look and told me to get to a doctor straight away. 'Leave your passport here and we'll issue your visa later when you're better.'

I staggered outside, wondering how on earth I was going to find a doctor. The best thing to do, I reasoned, would be to go to the head of the UNHCR. He was expecting me. He'd know what to do.

I found a taxi and, in my rudimentary Arabic, asked the driver to take me to the UNHCR office. Thankfully, he knew where it was.

The boss was a Frenchman. He'd never heard of me and, what's more, he wasn't at all interested in how bad I was feeling. 'If you were known to UNHCR, I'd have had a telegram from Geneva,' he told me. 'I have had no such telegram. Now I must ask you kindly to leave my office.'

'Well, can you at least tell me where I can get some medical assistance?'

'No, I cannot. Now, I tell you again, please get out.'

On my way out, the receptionist, who had overheard our exchange, gave me a frosty look. I told her I had bad abdominal pain and asked if *she* could tell me where to get medical assistance.

She sniffed. 'I am afraid I cannot 'elp you, mademoiselle.'

In the street the temperature was over 40 degrees and it was raining. I was desperately ill, without a passport or a visa, in a country where I knew no one. While I wondered what to do, a minibus crammed with passengers went by crawling slowly in the traffic. A man hanging half-in and half-out of the door saw me and said in English, 'Do you want help?'

'Yes. Yes, I think I do.'

He shouted to the driver. The bus stopped. 'What's the problem?'

'I think I have a medical problem.'

'Aieee. You'd better get in.' He asked some people to move and a small space appeared amongst the packed bodies. He patted the seat. 'Sit down and wait till we get to the piazza, then I'll see what I can do.'

The minibus continued on its journey, stopping now and again to pick up and let down passengers. At each stop, my Good Samaritan launched into a rapid rundown of the bus's destinations to waiting passengers, then collected their money when they boarded. He didn't ask me for a fare.

After several stops, we reached Place Rambo in the centre of town. As we got out, he said, 'This is not really my job, I was just filling in for a friend. Now, what can I do for you?'

'I'm in a really big mess. I came from Somaliland. I have no visa, my passport's at the airport and my stomach feels like it's going to burst.'

He listened sympathetically. 'It's probably some small thing. If you like, I can take you to my friends and they'll look after you.'

If I hadn't been feeling bad, I mightn't have been quite so willing to accept this offer from a man I didn't know but I was so sick I simply nodded.

We left the piazza and made our way through a maze of crowded streets. People stopped and stared with open curiosity at this man guiding a white woman through the throng. As we went along, he kept up polite conversation in good but accented English. He looked to be about thirty years old. If I thought anything about him at all it was that here was a person who had a generous spirit, for how many people would go to such trouble to help a stranger? I realised I didn't yet know his name.

'I should introduce myself,' I said. 'My name's Valerie.'

'Glad to meet you, I'm Ismael.'

We stopped outside a detached house in a somewhat shabby neighbourhood. A woman answered the door and a couple of little children peeked shyly from behind her dress. Inside, I could hear other children laughing and playing. Ismael introduced her as Asseya, his cousin's wife. She gave me a big smile of welcome and asked me to come in.

By this time I was close to collapse. Asseya took me to a quiet corner of the main room and told me to lie down on some cushions. She returned soon afterwards with some hot soup. Thoughtfully, they left me alone. In my weakened state, I would have been barely capable of carrying on a conversation anyway. I was vaguely aware of activity going on – children playing, the smell of cooking. I had the impression of a crowded, happy household. By late afternoon I was feeling much better. I suspect now that I was suffering from giardiasis, a type of gastro, from drinking bad water. The rain had stopped and Ismael asked me if I felt well enough to go to the airport.

He had borrowed a motorbike from a friend. With me riding pillion, he wove through the traffic to the immigration office. The people there seemed to know him, for he greeted them easily, smiling and cracking a joke or two. In no time at all, I had my passport with a nice new visa stamped inside.

Now that I was up to talking, Ismael asked me what I had been doing in Somaliland. I told him all about my work with the Ethiopians, Eritreans, Tigrinyas and other refugees.

'Why don't you ever think about doing work for the Afar?' he asked.

I told him that, apart from living briefly with the Afar at Afdera in northern Ethiopia, I knew very little about them.

He explained that the Afar had once been in the majority in Djibouti but, under the French, Issa people had been allowed to come into the country from northern Somalia and Ethiopia to help build the railway to Addis Ababa. They had gradually become the dominant group. The Issa were a more aggressive people than the Afar. Gradually, the Afar had become disenfranchised until now they were without power, work or money. There was trouble brewing between the two tribes and Ismael was worried that it might soon erupt into violence.

As I listened, I sensed that this was more than a polite history lesson for a foreign visitor. Ismael's passion was plain to see, in his gestures, in the tone of his voice, the glitter of his dark, expressive eyes. He told me he was a committed Afar patriot. He'd been brought up in Eritrea, where there were also many Afar, and had spent two and a half years in the Ethiopian navy as an engineer. In his early twenties he had come to Djibouti to join an Afar nationalist group, Mouvement Populaire de Liberté. He had lived in the bush teaching literacy classes to Afar children. He was deeply committed to making life better for the Afar.

I enjoyed our conversation. Ismael's description of the injustices that had befallen the Afar struck a chord with me. He was, I thought, an attractive man. He had a clear sense of justice, he was devoted to his people, and at the same time he was a bit of a joker, with a quirky sense of humour. I was a bit of a joker myself, so we had things in common.

We talked late into the night. He said he had to go out of town the next day, and asked if I would like to go with him. I declined, as I had to try to get my visa for Ethiopia.

In the morning I thanked the family for their hospitality. We exchanged addresses, Ismael puttered off on his borrowed motorbike and I made my way to the Ethiopian embassy. There, I was told that I would not be allowed to enter the country via train. The only way it could be done was for me to fly to Addis Ababa and see the Department of Information and Protocol. I knew that if I did that, there would be a security check, with a good chance of my past activities being discovered. Then I'd be in all sorts of trouble.

I tried wheedling. 'I only have enough money for the train from Djibouti to Dire Dawa,' I pleaded.

'We don't care about your money, it's government policy. No land entry.'

I went away defeated. Next day, I flew back to Hargeysa and told my friend in the UNHCR that I'd failed. I made one last effort, finding some Ogaden National Liberation Front fighters who were prepared to sneak me across the border. We went in without incident. They walked me part of the way towards Dire Dawa, but it was obvious that their hearts were not in it. They were afraid that they'd be caught by Ethiopian security. Before we'd gone very far, we turned back.

Back in the comfort of my friends' house in Mogadishu, it was time to take stock. I had been travelling rough and working hard for twelve months. I was feeling tired, and the governor of Somaliland was determined to make my life difficult. I felt that a chapter had ended. There was nothing really to keep me in this part of the world any longer. I said my goodbyes and boarded a flight for the long, meandering journey to Australia.

CHAPTER 8

Melbourne had become the preferred city for refugees from the Horn of Africa. I got a job with the Royal Women's Hospital and moved into a small one-room flat in Brunswick, sharing with a Somali girl. One of us slept in the bedroom while the other slept on the couch. There was rarely just the two of us there. Newly arrived refugees from Africa who were without a place of their own frequently dossed down on the floor while they looked for somewhere to live.

In August 1986, a few months after I'd arrived, Dottie came home from Saudi Arabia and moved in with us. There wasn't enough room for three, so Dottie and I took a two-room flat together in East Brunswick. This gave us more space but there was no lessening in the number of house guests. Dottie was very understanding about having to tread over sleeping bodies on the lounge room floor when she was getting ready to go to work.

I tried to work nights as much as possible, leaving the days free to spend on refugee matters. Under the letterhead of The Horn of Africa Committee, I'd write letters for people seeking residency, help them with legal problems, and any difficulties they were having with the authorities; I also put out a monthly newsletter about the situation back in their homelands.

I took agency work as well as doing my regular job at the Women's. I'd never learned to drive, so I had either to walk or take public transport everywhere. This could be time-consuming. For instance, it was an hour from my place to Clayton, where the Somalis held their meetings, so, what with my regular job and my refugee work, going to court, writing letters, attending meetings and so on, there was very little time left over for sleeping.

Dotti and I shared domestic duties. Dottie was a good cook, but I was quite happy to live on bread and lentils. I like nice food, but not enough to go to the trouble of cooking it. If poor Dottie wanted something tasty, she had to prepare it herself.

One day in early 1989 I went to a meeting at Footscray to meet some refugees who had just arrived from Djibouti. An Ethiopian girl came up to me and asked if I was Valerie Browning. 'I think I have a letter for you. I didn't bring it with me because I didn't know you'd be here.'

'Who's it from?'

'I don't know. A man gave it to me in Djibouti. He said if I came across a lady called Valerie Browning in Australia, to give it to her.'

It had been more than two years since I'd made my brief visit to Djibouti. I couldn't imagine who would be writing to me from there. I wrote down my address and a few days later the letter arrived. The original envelope had been marked simply 'Valerie Browning' with no address.

The letter was from Ismael. He said that he'd written to me several times and had never received a reply. This was the last letter he was ever going to write. If he didn't hear from me, he would not try again.

In Djibouti I'd given him the address of a Somali friend in Melbourne, as I hadn't known where I'd be staying. I'd since had a falling-out with this person. Every time one of Ismael's letters came, he'd thrown it straight in the bin.

I was mortified when I read the letter. Ismael had been so kind, looking after me when I was sick, helping me with my visa, inviting me to stay with his family, and it would have seemed I had snubbed him. He must have thought I was some sort of bighead.

I wrote back immediately, explaining what had happened. I thanked him again for his help and told him that the last thing I wanted to do was insult him. We exchanged a few letters after that. In one or two he hinted that he was interested in something more than mere friendship. I told him that I wasn't really interested in romance but I'd be happy to be a friend.

I was planning another trip to Sudan and Somalia soon. One day I was discussing it with Dottie when I had an idea. 'Do you know what, Bartram,' I said, 'I think I'll include Djibouti, and look up this fellow Ismael to say thank you.'

I went to Hargeysa and caught a flight to Djibouti. Ismael and his relatives welcomed me with their usual hospitality. For once in my life, I had no refugee camps to visit, borders to infiltrate, visas to arrange, reports to write: I was simply a tourist.

I enjoyed Ismael's company. He was easygoing, unruffled by the troubles and frustrations of life, of which he had seen more than most people. He spoke eight languages, and could slip in and out of different cultures with ease. Unlike many Muslim men, he could sympathise with points of view outside the narrow confines of Islam.

One day when we were sitting on Djibouti beach eating our way through a bunch of bananas, he said to me, 'I think I might marry you.'

'I beg your pardon?'

'Let's get married.'

I was so surprised, I babbled. 'You must have misunderstood me totally I'm very sorry you've probably got everything wrong because you think I'm a good westerner and you'd get some benefit out of me but you wouldn't I'm a hopeless westerner I've got no money people think I travel a lot but I have nothing in the bank why would you marry me?'

When I paused for breath, he said, 'I don't want your money. I'm asking you to live here.'

'That wouldn't work. I only spent a day with you two years ago. I hardly know you.'

He said something about love being like that. I told him he was mad. He said, 'I want a decision from you. Please give it to me.'

I was hardly a giddy girl losing her head due to love. I was 38 years old and I'd never had a love affair in my life. In the days that followed, I thought a lot about Ismael. He was nice, his friends were nice, I liked his family a lot. If I didn't marry now, I might never do it. There were definitely things to be said in favour of doing it. But there were many reasons against it too. Together, we went through them.

To begin with, I was a western woman. Western women had a different way of life from women in Djibouti. Sure, I'd spent a lot of time in Africa, but I was still nominally an Australian with all of the ingrained expectations of my upbringing.

And another thing: what if Ismael wanted to take another wife? The Koran permits up to four. I told him that I was strongly opposed to polygamy. I didn't understand how a marriage could work if there were other parties involved. For me, that would be impossible.

He assured me that he would respect my wishes. He had no intention of taking more than one wife.

Then there was the age difference. Ismael was four years

younger than me. But the biggest problem of all was our different religious beliefs. 'I'm a Christian,' I said. 'I'm not going to change to Muslim. Marriage wouldn't change my mind, so what are we going to do about that?'

He said, 'I wouldn't marry a person who doesn't hold God as central in their life. If you were a Hindu or a Buddhist, that would be different. The important thing is that we both worship the one God.'

I prayed repeatedly about this, asking for God's guidance. I never got the feeling that I shouldn't go ahead. All my married life, people have asked me why, as a Christian, am I married to a Muslim? I can't answer that except that I sincerely think that God has a plan that I don't totally understand.

I thought at one stage that I should consult my family. But then I thought, how could they help? They don't know this place or this culture. Slowly, I came to the conclusion that life in this part of the world was the way I should live.

A month after Ismael had proposed, I said yes. There was no ceremony. We simply went to the Sharia office and signed the registry. Ismael slipped a wedding ring onto my finger; it had his name engraved on the inside. His cousin had given it to us, as he was too poor to buy one himself.

I'd told Ismael that marriage was considered a pretty big thing in Australia and that I'd need to go home and tell my family. We had one more day together, then I flew back home to break the news.

My parents had retired to Nelson Bay, north of Sydney. I was nervous about telling them, especially my father. I didn't say anything for a day or two. Mother was fiddling about in the kitchen when I sidled up to her and said, 'I've got something to tell you.'

'I should think so, judging by that ring on your finger.'

We sat down at the kitchen table together and I told her all about Ismael. 'That's lovely, dear,' said Mother. 'It's what we wanted. Now, you'd better go and tell your father, he's in his study.'

'Why don't you tell him?'

'No, I'll make a lovely cup of tea, the way he likes it. You go and see him and I'll bring it in.'

I said, 'No, Mother, let me make the tea – you can tell me how, if you like – and you tell him.'

'That's not how the world works, my dear, I've told you before.'

I knocked on the study door before entering. As always with Father, I felt as if I were a child again, having to own up to some misdemeanour. I hedged around the topic for a few minutes, then blurted out my news.

'I suppose he's black, is he?' said Father.

'Well, he's African, yes.'

'Do you have a photograph?'

I showed him the one I'd brought with me. 'Hmm . . . I see. Are you going back there?'

'Yes.'

'Going to live there?'

'Yes.'

He handed back the photograph. 'All right, then.'

The rest of the family more than made up for Father's lack of enthusiasm. When my brothers and sisters found out, they organised a reception at my younger sister's place. Carolyn and her husband, Bob, live on a wheat farm at Old Junee near Wagga Wagga. It was a good old family get-together, the likes of which I hadn't seen for a decade or more. Everyone brought something to eat, and we all pitched in with the cooking – even me. There were speeches and lots of laughter and a proper ceremonial cutting of the wedding cake. Mother and Father and my whole family, with all of their children, were there. The only person missing was the groom.

After the wedding reception, I did the rounds of the brothers and sisters, staying with each in turn. The longer I was in Australia, the more nervous I became about returning to Djibouti. After four months, I thought, it's time, let's go and see what this marriage business is all about.

CHAPTER 9

Ismael had found a flat in the suburb of Engela, one of the poorest parts of Djibouti. It consisted of one room; the kitchen was a little alcove at the front with a Primus cooker on the floor; the bathroom was a tiny cubicle with a hole in the floor and you had to lift the door across to close it as the hinges had broken. Bathing was done with a bucket of cold water. We had a few broken-down TV sets to use as chairs, but mostly we sat on cushions on the floor. The walls had big cracks running through them. You had the feeling that the whole place could easily fall down.

We lived in absolute poverty. Ismael had a little business repairing electrical goods. He ran it the Afar way – if you didn't have the money right now, you could pay later. His customers made plenty of promises but they rarely settled their bills.

While I'd been in Australia, Ismael had found a church for me. He'd approached the Red Sea Mission Team and, when I arrived, he introduced me to a few of the members. One woman in particular, a Swiss, Maryanne, was quite friendly. She was a gentle, caring woman with four children. She visited me a few times, but she was busy with her own work and family, and coming to see me in the slums was quite a business for her. It soon became clear to me that if this marriage were going to work, I would have to put my whole heart into it. I had to become an Afar wife.

The first thing to change was my western clothing. I started to wear long dresses with long-sleeved blouses and a scarf over my head, as the locals did. Even so, I sometimes had to endure insults from men when I walked in the street, although Ismael's friends treated me with complete respect.

The Afar have a communal way of life. If someone has a bit of food or a place to sleep, they'll always share it with others who are less fortunate. Our little flat was always crowded with Ismael's friends. Sometimes there'd be half a dozen of them sleeping on the floor. Ismael called them his 'comrades', meaning that they were Afar nationalists like him. Many were involved with helping the community.

Being an Afar wife, it was up to me to cook for whoever happened to be around. Ismael would announce, 'She's cooking,' and I would think, cooking what? What can we buy? There's no money.

I had, of course, never been much interested in cooking and I was not instinctively good at it as some people are. My mother had taught me to make tuna with macaroni cheese, which the Afar thought was revolting. Ismael was no help. 'How can you think of putting fish and milk and cheese together?' he said. 'I've never tasted anything so disgusting in my life.'

That, and a few other similar critiques, made me quite depressed. I felt that I was failing in the most basic of wifely duties.

My best friend was our next-door neighbour, Aisha. She was a lovely, warm-hearted woman with thirteen children. She was always willing to have a cup of tea with me. She only spoke Afar but her sunny nature made up for the lack of common language. We didn't exactly have heart-to-heart conversations but, nevertheless, our relationship was a close one.

I could not yet speak any Afar, so I was surrounded by babble I couldn't understand. Some of Ismael's friends tried to talk to me in French, but I was hopeless at it.

It was hard to adjust to the Afar way of doing things. In the west, we talk about 'my space', or 'my time'. With the Afar, there is no such thinking. If you want to be by yourself, it won't be long before you have half a dozen people asking, 'Are you sick? Are you upset? Are you lonely? Can I sit with you?'

The Afar also have little concept of individual property. I'd never thought I was interested in material things until one day when all of my frustrations reached a flashpoint. As I recall, we were getting ready to go out when I found my hairbrush was missing. I threw a huge tantrum and Ismael was right in the firing line. 'I'm not going anywhere or doing anything until that hairbrush is found,' I screamed.

'You could use a comb,' he suggested.

'No, you don't understand. I'm not using a comb, I want my hairbrush.'

'Don't worry about it, it's sure to come back.'

'What do you mean, "come back"? It shouldn't have gone in the first place.'

I thought my whole life had collapsed over that hairbrush. A few days later it turned up. Ismael said, 'There you are, what were you worried about? Someone just borrowed it.'

If someone is showing off some new possession, they might say that they've got a nice watch, a nice this or a nice that. I no longer have a nice anything; that's all gone. I'm used to it now, but back then, as a new bride, it was difficult.

Ismael used some connections to get me a job at the government-run Hôpital Beltière. As part of my studies in Australia, I had done a midwifery course. I worked as a midwife in the delivery unit and looked after new mothers. The hospital was quite well equipped, with some good and some not-so-good doctors. Sometimes, helicopters would arrive carrying patients from rural areas. The women had always been circumcised at a young age. The clitoris and the labia had been cut away and they had been sewn up, leaving only a small opening. The vagina had grown together in the stitched area, so, the first thing to be done before delivering, was to make an incision to allow the baby to come out. In the rural areas, this would be done with a traditional birthing knife – *makiita* – or perhaps a razor blade. After the birth, the woman would be sewn up again. I had heard about female genital mutilation (FGM) but this was the first time I'd seen it. I was shocked that young girls could be mutilated in this way as a matter of course, and that no one seemed to think it was wrong.

A couple of months went by without my salary being paid. Whenever I asked about it, the hospital administration told me that the paperwork had not been completed but, not to worry, it would come through soon.

All in all, things were not going well. The yawning gap between Ismael's and my culture was beginning to show. Afar men do not show affection to their wives in public. Each partner in the marriage has their role to play and women are expected simply to get on with the job. The idea of praising me for a nice meal – and, despite my lack of experience, there were a few – or acknowledging that I'd gone to some trouble to look good, simply did not occur to Ismael. These are purely western concepts, I know, but I had not yet entirely shaken off my heritage. As much as I tried to be an Afar, I had nearly four decades of Australian upbringing to overcome. What with our poverty and the trying conditions in our home, I began to feel that I had made a very big mistake.

I'd left a little bit of money in Melbourne with Dottie. One day a few weeks after I had returned to Djibouti, I was feeling very depressed. I went to a travel agent and enquired about a one-way ticket to Australia. I had enough money to cover the fare but I thought that before I asked Dottie to send it, I should tell Ismael. For once, we had the flat to ourselves. I sat him down on the mattress on the floor and said, 'Listen, I've organised something.'

'Yes, what have you organised?'

'A ticket back to Australia.'

'We're going, are we?'

'Not you, me.'

'What? What do you mean?'

'I'm not coping. You haven't noticed. I don't speak any of these languages. I don't speak French, I don't speak Afar. I can never be by myself, there's always people around. I'm out. I'm not coping. I'm leaving.'

He looked at me steadily for a moment before replying. 'I think it's a bit early for this. I think we should try a little longer.'

Ismael was being Ismael – unflappable, even-tempered, tolerant – the very qualities for which I'd married him; while I was being my usual impetuous, impatient, assertive self. It was a foretaste of our married life to come. The softly-softly approach would not always win out, although on this occasion I'm glad to say that it did, for I hate to think how my life would have turned out without Ismael.

We agreed both to try a little harder. We were still poor, still living in the same conditions, everything remained the same, until, a few weeks later, there was an important change. I discovered I was pregnant.

About three months into the pregnancy I contracted pneumonia. I was in bad shape. I should have been at home in bed but I kept going to work each day because I was afraid that if I didn't, I'd never receive my salary. At home I'd sit up all night coughing up pus. We couldn't afford medicine, so Ismael brought me ginger *shahi* – tea – to try to stop the coughing. I never want to see another ginger *shahi* in my life.

After a month or so I gradually got my health back, which, considering what was to happen next, was just as well. Five weeks before the baby was due, I felt my first contractions. It was night-time. I assumed I had plenty of time before I'd need to go to the hospital, so I didn't wake Ismael. Then, a couple of hours after midnight, there was a sudden flood in the bed. My waters had broken.

I shook Ismael awake and told him it was time to go to the hospital.

He told me there was no way to get me there in the middle of the night. We'd have to wait until morning, when he could find a friend to take us in his car. As soon as it was daybreak Ismael fetched the car and off we went. It was a Friday, the Muslim day for rest and prayer. We waited a couple of hours for the Egyptian obstetrician on duty to see me. I knew that I was in for a difficult birth and that things were already at a critical stage. I could feel the baby's head near my side and what must have been a tiny hand down between my legs. When the doctor finally turned up, I told him that I didn't think the baby could come out the way it was lying.

'It might turn,' he said.

'It can't turn,' I said. 'Its hand is between my legs. You can do what you like with me, it won't turn.'

'Anyway,' he said, 'I can't do anything today, it's Friday. Wait until tomorrow and we'll see if we can get you into theatre.'

I said, 'I'm an older woman. This may be my only chance to have a baby. Please, I'm begging you.'

'I'm afraid I can't. It will be all right, I assure you.'

'What if the baby dies in the night?'

'I'll give you a stethoscope and you can listen to the heartbeat.'

It would have been obvious to a first-year medical student that the baby was coming. The correct procedure would have been to perform an emergency Caesarean immediately. As a medical professional myself, I knew that the decision not to act was a bad one but I was in such an emotional state that my normal feistiness deserted me. I was like any other first-time mother-to-be – scared, not thinking straight. Instead of fighting, I gave in and sat up all night in a state of terrified anxiety listening my baby's tiny heart beating inside me.

Next day, the theatre was booked out all morning. It wasn't until one o'clock that I was taken in. It was the same doctor. The anaesthetist gave me an epidural – a spinal injection that's meant to deaden all feeling from the waist down. I felt my legs go numb but I could still feel my abdomen. I told the doctor this. 'Never mind,' he said, 'it will work in a minute.'

To my horror, a few moments later he picked up a scalpel and swiftly made a horizontal cut. There was a searing pain like nothing I'd felt before in my life. I screamed and he looked up in surprise.

'I told you. It's not working,' I said.

The anaesthetist then gave me a general anaesthetic. When I was unconscious, the doctor got back to work.

During all of the waiting time the amniotic fluid had completely drained away, leaving a vacuum inside. This vacuum held the incision closed. Try as he might, for a long time the doctor could not open it, and when he did access the baby, he did not have the skill at manipulation to bring it out.

While the doctor was struggling, Ismael was watching anxiously through the half-open door. Whenever he asked what was wrong, someone assured him that everything was fine, the baby would be there at any minute.

An hour passed ... more ... and still my baby had not been born. It was obvious to everyone, if not my doctor, that something was terribly wrong. The nurses, who had been so optimistic before, now told Ismael that the baby would certainly not survive. Ismael's cousin, Asseya, went to find a white sheet in which to wrap the dead child. When she returned, they told her that she might as well get one for the mother as well.

The theatre nurses were my friends. One of them decided that she would have to do something or they would have a dead baby and a dead mother on their hands. Throwing her gown on the floor, she rushed out and commandeered the hospital's ambulance. She told the driver to take her to the chief obstetrician, a Somali. When they arrived at his home, they found that he'd moved. They raced to the new address and, thank God, he was there.

When he entered the operating theatre, he took one look at me and called for a scalpel. Without even pausing to put on a gown, he swiftly made a vertical incision and pulled the baby out. It was a girl. She wasn't breathing. They gave her a little slap on the bottom and still she did not breathe. They blew on her, wrapped her up and rubbed her tiny body to stimulate her, and still she remained lifeless. With time becoming critical, the doctor intubated her, putting an airway into her trachea. At last, her chest began to rise and fall. It had been five minutes before she drew her first breath. I had been opened up on the operating table for over three hours.

When I awoke from the anaesthetic and learned what had happened, my first thought was for my child. Five minutes is the very limit that a baby can go without breathing before suffering brain damage. I was certain that she would be severely handicapped.

She was a skinny little thing weighing just 2 kilograms. Because of what I'd been through, the nurses wanted to spare me from breastfeeding straight away and gave her sugar and water. Some women from the mission had heard about what was going on and had come to help. They insisted that I breastfeed. I'd only just come out from under the anaesthetic. I barely knew what was going on. Someone said, 'Come on, Valerie, you have to sit up.' The pain was horrible, but I struggled into a sitting position. They put the baby in my arms. She was affected by the anaesthetic too. She didn't want to feed. Still my well-meaning helpers persisted. I sat and cried while I tried to get this helpless little creature to take nourishment, but it just wasn't working. I know that mothers are supposed to go into a state of bliss when they breast-feed, but I must be honest and admit that I never enjoyed it.

I remained in hospital for the next two weeks. They kept antibiotic infusions running into me. Because I'd been opened up for so long, they were terrified of sepsis.

During those two weeks the baby's weight dropped 500 grams, to 1.5 kilograms. When she came home I was still terri-fied that something would be wrong with her. I made little paper charts, noting temperature, pulse rate, growth and weight, how much urine she passed and so on. I became convinced that she had cerebral palsy. For hours I studied the way she kicked, trying to decide whether her leg movements were unusually jerky. I'd listen to her cry, and try to tell if she was crying like a cerebral palsy child. I hardly slept. If she so much as whimpered in the night, I'd leap straight out of bed and run to where she lay on some cushions in a corner of the room. Ismael didn't seem to understand when I told him I was worried.

All of that wonderful maternal feeling that you're supposed to get seemed to be missing. I longed to talk to my mother or another woman. In my family, when one of my sisters had a child Mother would always go and spend time with her, fiddling around in the house, cooking, helping with the baby. I thought that if only one of my sisters were around, she could have told me,

'Don't worry, it's all right, I've been through that and it's okay.'

On the day before the birth, I'd said to Ismael, 'Do you realise that we don't have any clothes for this baby?'

'And so?'

'Well, can you go and find some so I don't have to take it out of the hospital naked?'

Ismael and his cousin had gone to the market and come back with a little shift, the cheapest thing they could find. Fortunately, Maryanne, my Swiss friend from the Red Sea Mission Team, came to see me and gave me some baby clothes. When she tried to reassure me, I thought, she doesn't understand, she doesn't see that this child's sick, that she's not normal.

I started to dream that I was the child's nurse. It must have had something to do with the fact that I'd worked in neonatal care with sick babies. After three months, one day I said to Ismael, 'I've had it, I can't continue. You've got to find this child's mother.'

He said, 'But you *are* the mother. You know you've been cut in your stomach. Don't talk like that. And who's breastfeeding?'

'I am, from sympathy.'

'It's not from sympathy, you're the mother.'

'I don't believe you. I'm tired. Please, Ismael, take the child.'

'No,' he said. 'Just wake up to yourself and stop being stupid.'

And, in the end, I did have to wake up to myself. Gradually, I calmed down and realised that I didn't have to keep all these charts, there was no doctor asking me for reports on her condition; she was a perfectly normal girl child, with milk-coffee skin, slightly built, like her mother, and beautiful like her dad.

We called her Aisha, after Ismael's mother.

I took a month off from work. I was afraid to take longer because I still had not received a cent of my salary. I thought that if I didn't turn up, they'd simply take me off the books and I'd never be paid. When I went back to the hospital, I took Aisha with me each day and kept her in a basket in the laundry. If she woke up, I could hear her from the delivery room. Sometimes I'd be in the midst of assisting a birth when she'd start to cry. I'd mentally plead with the mother: For heaven's sake, woman, push that thing out. Can't you hear my baby crying? Aisha's looking for breast milk. Sometimes, though, Aisha had to wait quite a while before I could attend to her.

When I'd become pregnant, I had told Ismael that if I had a girl I wouldn't stand for her being circumcised. I made it clear that if he insisted, it would be the end of our marriage. I don't think that he quite understood at that time what a barbaric ritual FGM was, although he certainly does now.

Ismael was his usual tolerant self. He said, 'Okay, if that's the way you think, that's fine.'

I made sure that his family knew my views as well. Ismael's sister, Hasna, fell pregnant at about the same time. She told me, 'I heard your message and I agree with you. If you have a girl, she should not have this FGM and neither will my girl, if I have a girl. I'll support you if my mother doesn't agree.' Fortunately, it never came to that. Ismael's mother sent word via Hasna that she would not oppose us.

Hasna was Ismael's full sister. They were both from his mother's second marriage. She lived with her husband in another town, Obock, 120 kilometres away from Djibouti City. She and I got on really well together. We were allies. We were going to bring up our children together. However, fate had other things in store for us.

There was one further drama to come with Aisha. One night, when she was about nine weeks old, she began to have difficulty breathing. By daybreak she was practically choking and was running a high fever. I was beside myself with worry. I said to Ismael, 'She's going to die, I know it.'

'We'd better take her to the hospital. You know the doctors, go to them.'

We had no money for a taxi, so we took it in turns to carry her, running through the town on the twenty-minute journey to the hospital. One of the kindly French doctors diagnosed pneumonia. He ordered two different types of medicine and told us to give them to her back at home. He said that if she got worse, we were to bring her straight back and they'd put her on oxygen.

We had no money to pay for the prescriptions. Ismael asked his relatives to help him, but they could only come up with enough for one of the medicines, an antibiotic. So, we took her home and ministered to her, and worried and cried, and prayed, each of us in our own way; and, through the grace of God, my miracle child, Aisha, lived.

CHAPTER 10

Djibouti is a tiny country of about half a million people situated right on the southern entrance to the Red Sea. It's mostly stony desert, with some scattered plateaux and highlands. In the third century BC, Ablé tribesmen migrated there from Arabia. Until recent years, their descendants, the Afar, roamed through Djibouti, Eritrea and Ethiopia at will, never bothering about borders or national sovereignty.

The French acquired Djibouti in 1858 through a treaty with the ruling Sultans. They called it French Somaliland. The Afar were the predominant group until the turn of the century, when the French decided to build a railway line from the port of Djibouti to Addis Ababa. The Afar had no desire to give up their nomadic way of life to work on the railway, so the French imported Issa people from Somalia to do the job.

In 1967 there were about 20,000 Issa in Djibouti and the rest were Afar. Nevertheless, in that year the French renamed it the Territory of the Afar and Issa. In 1977 it became an independent nation and took on the same name as its capital, Djibouti.

Ismael describes the two groups as 'cool people and hot people' and that sums up perfectly the difference between them.

The Afar way is to live and let live; the Issa are aggressive and warlike. When Djibouti was granted independence, the Afar leader, Ahmed Dini, had the opportunity to become the first president. Instead, he stepped aside and allowed the Issa candidate, Hassan Gouled Aptidon, to take the position. Ahmed Dini took on the less powerful role of prime minister. I met Mr Dini several times because of Ismael's work with the Afar. He used to say he'd made a huge mistake. He'd wanted Djibouti to be the first African democracy, with all people living together in peace. When he stood aside and allowed the Issa man to be number one, the Issa found the hole in the fence, as it were, and took over. By the time I was living there, there were about 170,000 Afar out of a population of 470,000. The Afar had been totally disenfranchised, without work, power or money. All of the important government ministries – Interior Affairs, Education, Defence, Foreign Affairs, Commerce – were controlled by Issa. In the capital, many Afar had gravitated to a slum called Arhiba, next to our suburb, Engela. They lived in squalid conditions, without work, discriminated against whenever they had dealings with authority. Many were starving.

Now and then, there would be peaceful demonstrations in Arhiba demanding a better deal from the government. Soldiers would often break them up with tear gas. Ismael and his friends would go into the thick of things and help tear-gas victims away to safety. They'd bathe their streaming eyes with water, and take the worst cases, or those who'd been otherwise injured, to hospital. After one of these demonstrations, Issa soldiers swept through Arhiba, forcing their way into homes and arresting people. Ismael, along with many others, was taken to a prison outside the city. I was working night shift at the hospital when it happened. When I came home, some of his friends told me he'd been arrested. I was worried. I didn't know what to expect. Was he going to be charged with some crime? Would he be just kept in prison indefinitely? I had no idea when I'd see him again.

He was released a day later. The police took the prisoners in a truck to the outskirts of the city and let them out, leaving them to make their way back home.

Another time, Ismael took himself off to Obock to see his sister and didn't come back for two months. I never heard from him, so I had no idea what he was doing or whether he was alive or dead. One night I was lying in bed feeling very sorry for myself. I was sobbing my heart out. Little Aisha got up from her mattress and toddled over to me. She placed her hands one on either side of my head and gently rocked me. It was a wonderful, calming gesture from a mere toddler. We have an amazing bond, Aisha and I. She has always been old beyond her years.

Tensions between the Afar and the Issa were becoming more serious by the day. In the north of the country, guerilla fighters from FRUD, the Front for the Restoration of Unity and Democracy, attacked and killed some Issa soldiers. In the pre-dawn darkness of 18 December 1991, the Issa took their revenge.

At about three a.m, I was woken by the sound of gunfire. I shook Ismael and told him that something was wrong. Blearily, he grumbled, 'Oh, woman, you always dream horrible dreams. Stop it, go back to sleep.'

I said, 'It's gunfire, Ismael. I won't sleep until you tell me who's firing the guns, then I'll go to sleep.'

Then he really woke up. The gunfire was coming from the direction of Arhiba. Ismael left the house in a hurry and came back about an hour later. 'It's very bad,' he said. 'Very, very bad. There's no retaliation. They're killing Afar. I must go back. You take the baby to Aisha next door and run to the hospital. There'll be huge casualties.'

I did as he said. Within half an hour, the first minibus arrived, loaded with injured and dying. Blood was dripping out the door as if it were a butcher's van. There were people with terrible injuries. A woman had her breast hanging by a thread of skin. One boy's leg was completely severed. These wounds had not been caused by bullets. The soldiers must have used explosives as well.

For the next 24 hours I did not stop working. I was staunching wounds in the corridors to try to stop the blood flow before I pushed the victims in to the doctors. The French doctors were heroic. They worked and worked without pausing to eat or sleep. Without them, hundreds more would have died. Some Issa nurses refused to do anything. When I saw them just standing around, something inside me snapped. 'Get up and work,' I demanded. 'You don't stop.'

'These people are rubbish. Let the rubbish die.'

'No! You don't let them die. You've forgotten what you are. You're nurses.'

No matter how hard I tried to persuade them, they absolutely refused to work.

This night of infamy became known as the Arhiba Massacre. Sixty-six people were killed. In their grief, the people of Arhiba erected a memorial to their martyrdom.

Reconciliation is part of Afar culture. If there has been a disagreement, you must not carry it further. You have to talk it out, using an intermediary if necessary. FRUD had already turned its back on the Afar way. Ismael and his friends went in to Arhiba to try to persuade people that fighting was not the answer. They went from house to house pleading with ordinary men and women, the religious leaders, to be Afar. They implored them, 'Don't cry, don't show the government you're sad, forget it, let us go forward in peace.'

Who knows what might have happened had the people listened? Perhaps even then there could have been a rapprochement, except for one final, brutal act of provocation. A few days after the memorial to the dead had been built, a government bulldozer, protected by soldiers, bulldozed it into the ground. This was the end as far as the community was concerned. They told Ismael and his friends, 'There can be no peace. They have burnt us in our beds, killed innocent people, and now they've insulted their memory. We have to go to war.'

I had not seen Ismael for a month. I will never forget how he looked the day he came home. He was exhausted and I could see defeat written on his face. 'We've failed,' he said. 'I'm leaving tonight and going to Ethiopia. We're going to find a way.'

'What about me and the baby?'

'You'll have to follow, after I get set up.'

'Follow, how? You must be clear about this, Ismael, I have to know what's going on. You can't just pack your bags and go.'

'I don't know. You'll get a message.'

There wasn't much I could do. I kept on going to work with Aisha and tried to carry on as if everything were normal. There was one good thing: at last they began to pay my salary and I received a year's back pay, which I put in the bank. One morning about six weeks after Ismael had left, the man from the corner shop came to me saying that I had a telephone call. It was Ismael. He sounded edgy, and harassed, as though he were under strain. He said I should get a visa and come with Aisha to Ethiopia. I was full of questions but he cut me short. 'Telephones are bad,' he said, 'we don't discuss. I'll call again in a few days.'

By that time I was ready. I didn't have much to pack, just a couple of dresses, a few baby things and that was it. There was no trouble with a visa. That old *persona non grata* edict had been long forgotten. When I landed in Addis, there was my husband, handsome and nonchalant as ever. It was wonderful to see him.

We did not kiss or embrace. Ismael still never showed any sign of affection towards me in public; it would have been regarded as extremely strange behaviour. It's different with children, though. He took Aisha in his arms and cuddled her while we drove into the city in a taxi.

Ismael had taken a room in the Taitu Hotel. It was a run-down place. The paint was peeling, the bed sagged wearily, the plumbing was a challenge, but it was reasonably clean and, really, no worse than our old place in Djibouti. I barely had a chance to talk to Ismael about what he had been doing all this time. Later that same day we went to another hotel, the Extreme, to meet with other Afar patriots who had fled Djibouti.

We greeted them in the traditional way: they kissed my hand, then I kissed theirs and they again kissed mine. There were the usual polite enquiries after my health and Aisha's, then one said, 'It's good that you've come. We want you to form an organisation.'

I said, 'What are you talking about?'

'A humanitarian organisation. You know how to do it. The government is bent on burning the Afar out of Djibouti. Unless FRUD has support, we cannot go ahead with the war.'

War? FRUD? What support? Did he say 'we'? There were a dozen questions I wanted to ask but, before I could open my mouth, Ismael said in English, 'I've told them we agree. Don't say you don't agree.'

Still not sure what I was agreeing to, I said, 'Okay, we'll try.'

Djibouti was embroiled in a full-scale civil war, with FRUD on one side and the Issa army on the other. Ismael did not wish directly to support the fighters but he was determined to do what he could for Afar victims of the conflict. His idea was to buy food and medicines and distribute them inside Djibouti.

We wrote and called on aid agencies and European embassies in Addis Ababa to try to raise money. In early 1993, 32 people including Aisha and me gathered at the isolated little river valley of Sidiica Mangela, where the borders of Ethiopia, Eritrea and Djibouti meet. It had been arranged by FRUD. Many of those present were FRUD leaders who had been fighting in Djibouti. It was early summer. Temperatures daily soared to 45 or 50 degrees. For five days, we sat in the shade of acacia trees discussing the way forward for the Afar people. Some of the local women prepared food for us. We ate *ga'ambo* and milk, and occasionally goat. At night, we slept on the ground under the stars. Although my Afar was still poor, I was able to understand the gist of what was going on. The result of that historic gathering was the formation of the Djibouti Relief Association.

A few weeks later we all met again at a place called Ra Ra, not far from Sidiica Mangela, to assess progress. Ra Ra was so isolated that motor vehicles called only rarely. Ismael had arranged for a friend to come and collect us in his car after five days, and take us to Bisidero in Eritrea. After the meeting finished everyone dispersed, leaving Ismael and me. Aisha was not with us this time; she was being looked after by relatives in Eritrea. We waited all day for our lift but it did not arrive. That night was unbelievably hot. The air hummed with the high-pitched whine of millions of mosquitos trying angrily to penetrate our nets. I was missing Aisha terribly. I woke up feeling that if I had to spend another day sitting around waiting, I'd go mad.

By the time we'd finished our breakfast of bread and lentils with a glass of sweet *shahi*, the car still had not come. It was 80 kilometres from where we were to the main road to Bisidero. I said to Ismael, 'I can't wait any longer. Come on, let's start walking.'

He said, 'We can't go, it's too hot. It's dangerous.'

One of my many character defects is that once I get it in my head to do something, I won't let anything stand in my way. I knew it was too hot. I was, after all, from Australia, where every schoolchild is aware of the danger of heading off into the desert without proper precautions. But I kept nagging Ismael until he gave in.

He had arrived at the meeting with a new pair of shoes. Because we'd expected to be travelling by car, he'd swapped them with a friend who had a lot of walking to do, for a pair of old ones. Those shoes should have been thrown away long ago. The uppers were falling apart and one sole was missing, forcing Ismael to walk with a limp.

It was mid afternoon by the time we decided to leave. We carried some bread and about 4 litres of water each. Our route led us along a gravel road, more like a track, over which our car would have to travel. So, if the car turned up, we'd meet it along the way.

Towards nightfall, when we'd travelled about 20 kilometres, we came across an Afar camp of half a dozen *deboitas*. They welcomed us, gave us some *ga'ambo* and refilled our water containers. At dawn next morning we set off once more, savouring the relative coolness while the sun was still low. All too soon, it rose above the horizon, a shimmering white orb beating down mercilessly out of a cloudless sky. The landscape wavered. The perspiration ran in rivulets inside our clothing. We plodded onwards, putting one foot in front of the other automatically. We saw no cars.

At lunchtime, we stumbled off the track into a dried-up river bed. We ate our bread and finished the last of the water. Ismael estimated that we had another 40 kilometres to go. We conferred. We could wait where we were for a vehicle to come along, or keep going.

I worried that it might be days before a car came; I was all for pressing on. While we'd been eating our miserable meal, black clouds had been forming overhead. There was a tympani roll of thunder and solid sheets of rain poured down as if someone had trained a fire hose on us. Soon the road became a river. Ismael, in his broken-down footwear, was making heavy going of it. His feet were blistered and, because of his uneven gait, he had developed a searing pain in his back. I would forge ahead, and have to stop and wait now and then for him to catch up.

Each burst of thunder was accompanied by a jagged tongue of lightning. I could see and hear it striking the ground all around. The desert was completely flat, with not even a small hill as far as we could see. We were the highest things in it. I was terrified.

At nine o'clock at night the rain stopped. Everything we carried was soaking wet. We wrapped our one sodden blanket around us and huddled together on the ground, shivering with cold. Somehow I managed to get some fitful sleep. At six a.m., we got to our feet and, moving stiffly at first, hobbled off down the road once more. At eleven, we reached the outskirts of a small village. We were exhausted and ravenously hungry, having not eaten anything since lunchtime the day before. A man who was herding some camels greeted us and offered us some *doma*, an intoxicating drink made from the sap of the doma palm. I accepted gratefully. The effect it had on me was immediately to give me mouth sores right down my throat, which made eating painful for the next seven days.

We both had trouble walking the final hundred metres to the village, partly due to the *doma* and partly because of our tiredness. The people there knew Ismael. They made us comfortable in one of their huts and gave us a meal of pasta. I've eaten a lot of pasta in my life but this was the best meal I've ever had. While we were eating, they sent a man on a bicycle to ride 10 kilometres and fetch us a car.

Ever since that hellish walk, Ismael has suffered from sciatica. He has been prescribed medicine for it but we've never been able to afford it. When the pain becomes too bad, he goes to a traditional healer who gets him to strip to his underpants, buries him in the hot sand, then rubs him with oil and gives him a massage. This cures Ismael for a while, but it's something he'll probably have to live with for the rest of his life.

During the march, Ismael said on more than one occasion that we should have waited, and that I was too impatient. I'm afraid that my impetuousness has not lessened with the passage of time. I've always been happy to take risks without giving too much thought to danger. I still tend to make decisions instantly, relying on instinct as much as logic. Of course, I regret that particular decision, as it led to Ismael being ill but, on the whole, I think I'm usually pretty right in deciding what we should do, or who we should or should not deal with.

Back in Ethiopia I began lobbying Médecins sans Frontières (MSF) for assistance with medical supplies. By early 1994, they were becoming interested. A man and a woman from MSF came along to our next meeting at Ra Ra. They had a long march from Bure to get to us. When the meeting ended they asked Ismael if they could return not to Ethiopia but to Eritrea. Perhaps it was the thought of that hard slog on foot that put them off. Ismael was never one to worry about border formalities. He told them, sure, he'd take them to Eritrea. They could go to Assab on the Red Sea coast and catch a bus from there.

There was a checkpoint outside the town of Assab, manned by mostly Afar soldiers. Ismael gave them his usual cheery greeting, as if he'd known them all his life. They chatted for a while and laughed at a couple of jokes. Then he gave them a wave, and off he and his MSF companions went. At Assab, he saw his friend the governor and explained how the French people had come into the country. The governor gave them a *Laissez Passer*. I heard later that when they left the country to re-enter Ethiopia, there was no trouble.

The war had recently ended and Eritrea was on the verge of being recognised as an independent state. Thousands of Afar in northern Djibouti, along with FRUD forces, were blockaded by the Issa army from any help from the south. At Sidiica Mangela, the meeting had decided to try to base operations in Eritrea, accessing northern Djibouti from there. The Ethiopians had already refused us permission. Ismael, Aisha and I went to the capital, Asmara, where Ismael had a series of meetings with government officials, seeking permission to take food assistance across the border. The Minister for the Interior shoved him on to the department which looks after aid. They shoved him right back, and the minister was suddenly unavailable. I had naïvely thought that, because of my former links with the EPLF, they'd help. It was clear that they had no intention of doing so.

While we were in Asmara we heard that Professor Fred Hollows was going to open the new factory which had been built to manufacture artificial lenses. Ismael, Aisha and I went along to watch the ceremony. Isaias Afeworke was there and Fessa-haie, and another face I recognised – the man who had been my guide when we'd walked to within 4 kilometres of occupied Asmara. He was Afeworke's bodyguard.

I pushed my way through the crowd, with my husband holding one hand and my child the other. I wanted to introduce them to my former comrades. I remember I was smiling as I approached them. The bodyguard stared at me without expression, then deliberately stamped on my foot with his heavy military boot. Ismael muttered, 'Come on, we're getting out of here,' and pulled me away. The EPLF, it seemed, had long memories.

We decided to fly back to Assab, then return to Addis. At the airport, we found that the plane was full, even though we had confirmed tickets. 'Never mind,' said Ismael. 'We'll go by sea.'

At the port of Massawa, there was a ship going to Assab. When the immigration people checked our passports before boarding, they discovered a problem: there were no entry stamps.

'How did you come here?' the officer asked.

'We came from Assab,' said Ismael.

'But how did you enter Eritrea in the first place?'

'Look,' said Ismael. 'That's not your problem. We came from Assab to Asmara, we want to go back to Assab. If you have any doubts, leave it to the immigration people there.'

They conferred for a few minutes then, to my astonishment, they agreed. I have seen Ismael talk his way around obstructive officials many times. He's amazing. He always knows exactly how to deal with them: he either bullies them, or bamboozles them with technicalities; or else beguiles them with jokes and flattery. He seems to know instinctively which tactic to use.

The passage to Assab was a rough one. For two days and a night, Aisha and I were seasick. We lay in our beds wishing we could die. Ismael, on the other hand, had a wonderful time. He'd spent his childhood in Assab, fishing and swimming in the Red Sea, and later he'd been in the navy. He passed the time talking to the ship's officers and enjoying every minute of being at sea.

From Assab, we went to Harsili, about 20 kilometres away, where I met my mother-in-law, Aisha, for the first time. Ismael's father had died when Ismael was fifteen and his mother had remarried. Her second husband had also died. She'd had a hard life bringing up five children. I already knew Hasna and Ismael's half-brother, Mohammad, from Djibouti. Now I got to know his half-sisters, Fatuma and Mayram. We all liked one another immediately. My mother-in-law was a lovely, warm-hearted woman with a great sense of humour. The first thing she said when we met was, 'Why did you marry this hopeless street boy? You're a nice girl; this wretched boy is so unreliable and you've gone and married him.'

She followed this with peals of laughter. There was a lot of laughter and a lot of love in that house. I immediately felt accepted.

Like so many poor Afar, their lives would be touched by tragedy. Ismael's mother died in 1997. Hasna, Mayram and Mohammad would all die of TB – three needless deaths which would never have happened in a developed country. Ismael's one remaining sibling, Fatuma, lives in Harsili, where she brought up Hasna's daughter as well as eight children of her own. She now has more than twenty grandchildren and ekes out a living as a goat herder.

We couldn't stay for long. We had to get back to Ethiopia and start work. Ismael went to his friend the governor once again. Armed with the papers he gave us, we had no trouble at all passing through the border.

At Sidiica Mangela, the clan leaders had identified the ways in which we hoped to help the Afar in Djibouti. The top priority was health. The Afar were subject to all of the diseases that afflict poor people all over Africa. There were six major issues affecting preventable death – diarrhoea, fever, poor maternal diet leading to deficient anaemia, coughing and spitting, misuse of medicines, and sexually transmitted diseases. As well, many were being injured in the fighting. The elders had decided we would need to find medicine, recruit health workers to administer it, and organise some way of getting supplies into Djibouti whilst avoiding the Issa army. That was the plan. It was up to Ismael and me to make it happen.

CHAPTER 11

It quickly became obvious that it was going to be very difficult to obtain funding from the usual aid agencies. A few expressed interest, but the only one that gave us concrete help initially was Médecins sans Frontières. This French organisation had been set up to make short-term responses to conflict situations. They were, and still are, a real gung-ho, can-do organisation. They weren't bothered at all by the fact that we would be operating without the agreement of either the Ethiopian or the Djibouti governments. They agreed to contribute medicines.

We used some of my money from Djibouti; my parents and some of my brothers and sisters also contributed funds from Australia, and we ended up with a team of ten camels. They were a motley collection, some long past their prime, with moth-eaten fur, scars from battles with other camels, some with bad teeth and most with bad tempers to match. One was named Ayatollah after Ayatollah Khomeini, because he was so ugly. His lips sagged dreadfully. Another was Yokyok, which was the nickname of one of our health workers. This wasn't an insult, as the Afar have the highest regard for camels.

The Afar have a system of communication, *daagu*, which has

evolved over centuries of nomadic existence. If Afar meet on a walking track, they will greet one another in the name of God. They will ask after each other's health and the health of their family, how the animals are, how is the weather situation where they have come from. One might ask, 'Did you see anything unusual in your direction?'

The other might say he saw a camel. 'He was not grazing, he was fretting. He didn't look like he knew this area. His head was high.'

'What marks did the camel have?'

'Oh, he had such and such a mark.'

They'll pass on the news that there's a fretting camel coming in this direction. This is how they'll find their lost camel. They use *daagu* to get help for sick people, or to pass on information about the spread of sickness; all sorts of information. Recently, there was a nasty incident in which some British aid workers were hijacked in Afar. That news came to us via *daagu* within a matter of hours. We knew who'd done it, where and how, and what vehicle was involved. When we tried to pass the information on to the Ethiopian government, they wouldn't believe it. The whole thing was resolved when Ismael came to Addis and gave the information to the British government's Department for International Development, DFID. Under pressure from the British, the government acted and the aid workers were released.

Through *daagu*, we learned where our medical supplies were needed. It might be an outbreak of diarrhoea in a certain area, or we'd hear of people being wounded in a clash with the Issa army somewhere. The illnesses were those with which I'd become familiar during my time in Africa – malaria, ear, eye, skin and chest infections, diarrhoea and so on.

Because of his bad back, Ismael couldn't walk long distances, so I was in charge of the camel trains. We'd load the beasts with medical supplies at Bure, three hours' walk from the border with Djibouti, then slip across at night. There'd be about ten people in the group. We'd often walk for two or three days, living off food given to us by the locals. I couldn't ride a camel. I'd tried once in northern Sudan, and the rocking motion nearly broke my back, so I always walked. I could do 40 or 50 kilometres in a day easily; the only time I had difficulty was on steep descents. Once we had to climb up an escarpment of dried lava flows called the Dacca Plateau. I got to the top with no trouble but the only way I could get down the other side was to bump along on my bottom. My comrades, dancing along as nimbly as goats, thought it was hilarious, but I must admit I had a hard time seeing the funny side.

We lived with the constant worry that we'd be discovered by the Issa army. While returning from one trip deep inside Djibouti, we were just leaving a village called Randa when we learned that the soldiers were right behind us. We had to make a forced march for the border. It was hellishly hot. We walked for fifteen hours without pause. Every time I begged my companions to rest, they said, 'No, there's no peace, keep walking.' We carried sugar in our pockets and some water in containers. We'd take a lick of sugar and a gulp of water as we went. That was the only sustenance we had.

When we finally made it to safety at Eli Daar, on the other side of the Ethiopian border, I collapsed. My feet were blistered, I had blood under my toenails and my legs were swollen from the knees down. Later, my big toenails fell off.

If we had been caught, I have no doubt I would have been killed. A FRUD fighter who'd been captured by the Issa and escaped, had seen my photograph among the wanted posters on the wall of an army command post. I had seen ample evidence of the Issa's bloodlust. One of my tasks on these trips was to document the atrocities they committed as they rampaged through the countryside. They killed a teenage boy by cutting his leg off and hanging it like a hunk of meat in a tree, leaving him to bleed to death. I saw a house in which they'd murdered a relative of one of the FRUD commanders. They slit his neck and swung him around until they painted the whole house with blood. They killed an old man by chopping the back of his neck as he knelt on his prayer mat. I interviewed women who'd been pack-raped by a dozen men. They were horribly injured in body and mind. These atrocities were meant to make people afraid of supporting FRUD. In some cases it worked, but mostly it only made people more determined than ever. I carefully noted down the details of each incident with names, dates, and locations. When I got back to Ethiopia, I sent reports to the BBC Africa Service and to Amnesty International.

I think it must have been about this time that Hamid, one of the FRUD leaders, gave me my nickname: Maalika. In Arabic, it means 'Queen'. Somehow, it's stuck ever since. Most Afar know me as Maalika rather than Valerie.

We had another very close call at Koranga on the Red Sea coast. As I mentioned before, the soldiers had been concentrating their efforts in the FRUD heartland north of Djibouti. Anyone travelling north was stopped and their money taken. Consequently, food supplies were not getting through and the people were starving.

We had just distributed food relief in Koranga when we got word that the Issa were driving a FRUD force towards us along the coast. Reconnaissance planes were spotting the guerillas from the air and directing the Issa ground troops to them. Again, the Issa's tactics were to drive a wedge between the people and FRUD by creating fear. Whenever they took over a town, they would go on a rampage of raping and looting. The whole town mobilised, abandoning their homes and possessions to flee into the countryside. My companions and I headed for the border, a forced march of about seven or eight hours. The last five hours were through a hellish landscape of rocky desert called the Buyya Rocks. We were stumbling with exhaustion by the time we reached the border but, once again, we had managed to stay ahead of the Issa army. In the confusion of getting away I left behind my shoulder bag. It contained the only piece of jewellery, apart from my wedding ring, that I possessed – my Aunt Ethel's engagement ring, which Mother had passed on to me after I'd got married. I think that was when God finally really taught me not to worry about possessions.

We lived a lot of the time in a friend's house in Eli Daar which was close to the border with Djibouti. When we were in Addis, we continued to live in the Taitu Hotel for the first few months of operations. Then we moved into a rented house in the suburb of Shola Makananya. Most other houses in the street were made of mud brick. This one had solid stone walls, a concrete floor and a tin roof. It was surrounded by a high stone wall with an iron gate. A small round table, one bed, and two chairs were all the furniture we owned. Cooking was done on a couple of Primus stoves on the kitchen floor.

Up to twenty Afar shared our accommodation at times. Sick boys would sometimes be brought down from the north, where there were only two hospitals for more than a million people. I'd try to treat their illnesses myself or else I'd look after them until I could get them to hospital.

Sometimes I looked after wounded FRUD fighters. One of these was a young man called Abdurahman. Abdurahman was about 22 or 23. He'd been fighting at Randa, a little way inland from the coast of Djibouti, when he was shot in the spine. His comrades had taken him across the border to a hotel in Awash, then left him in order to hurry back into battle. We got the message that there was a wounded boy in a back room of the hotel. When we found him, the whole of his backside had rotted out and was infested with maggots. He was a paraplegic, unable to move from the waist down. I cleaned him up as best I could, stuffed cloths into the gaping holes in his backside, and took him home to Addis.

Abdurahman told me what had happened. His best friend had been shot in the abdomen. He had taken a long time to die in terrible agony. Abdurahman now would wake up night after night screaming with the same nightmare. I'd sit with him and calm him down, and tell him, 'Abdurahman, it's over. It's over. You've got to get it out of your brain. You've got to believe that we're with you and the world will go on.'

He found that hard to accept. At night, he'd say, 'Maalika, I don't want to sleep, stay with me tonight, I don't want to see him again.'

I'd bring my mattress in and bed down beside him. If I had to go away, he'd plead with me, 'Maalika, I don't want you to leave, I want you to be with me all the time.' But I couldn't be there all the time, and while I was away he'd be in such a state that he'd refuse to eat.

Someone had to help him out of his wheelchair and wash him and help him with the toilet. Paraplegics have all sorts of special difficulties, and we weren't really equipped to deal with either his physical or his mental trauma. Eventually, Abdurahman developed TB in the spine. He'd been with us for three years when it became obvious that he was dying. We knew he was from Assab. Ismael phoned some friends and asked them to try to find his relatives and pay the bus fare for one of them to come down. We told Abdurahman that they were coming and pleaded with him to hold on.

They found his family, and a brother was delegated to make the journey. Abdurahman managed to live until he came and then, when he saw him, he gave up. Right at the end, he called out for his mother. I said to him, 'Wait, I'm going to get your mother on the phone.' His eyes opened and he gave me a strange, wonderful look – a look of absolute love. He grabbed me around the neck and pulled me down on top of him and whispered, 'This is my mother.'

Then he died in my arms. Abdurahman was the closest thing to a son I'd ever had.

I started training people to become health workers. They were all boys from Djibouti. Some had had a bit of first aid training, some had none at all. I was able to teach them simple things, such as how to vaccinate and to treat the common illnesses that we encountered in Djibouti. It's amazing how much you can teach an unqualified person in a short time. For instance, to stop diarrhoea you can make a rehydration fluid from a litre of water, a handful of sugar and three pinches of salt. You shake it up and let the patient drink it. Or you can make a cereal rehydration fluid out of a cup of flour, eight cups of water, sugar and salt. That makes a gluey porridge which is like cement in the bowel and stops the diarrhoea. With skin diseases, it's often just a matter of good hygiene. We taught them what food is necessary if a woman is pregnant or breastfeeding, and many other bush medicine techniques.

Our health workers were all volunteers. They went in with the camel trains, ran the gauntlet of the Issa army, lived a hard and dangerous life and were never paid a cent. They did it for their people, for that is the Afar way.

I became especially close to one health worker, Ahmed Ali Angaddu. He was a fine boy, driven by fierce patriotism. He and

I had a dream that one day we'd write everything that I'd taught him, in a book. It would be a manual for health workers throughout the Afar territories.

Now we have that manual, but Ahmed did not live to see it. He was by himself deep in the hinterland, in an area of chronic food shortages, when we got word that he was ill and did not have anything to eat. I suspect that he had malaria. Afar volunteers tried to reach him from the Ethiopian side and from within Djibouti but, before they got to him, he had starved to death.

I grieved as if a member of my own family had died. But such setbacks only reinforced my will to keep going. I never for a moment thought of giving up.

There never seemed to be enough time to do everything. Our house at Shola Makananya was always full of young men who'd been messed up by the war. I used to cook up massive amounts of pasta and *shiro* – ground chickpeas mixed with spices – for them. One night, I came home and counted 30 bodies sleeping on the floor. As well as looking after Aisha and Ismael, the ever-present house guests, and training health workers, once every two months I wrote what I called 'Updates' on an old Corona typewriter. They contained news of our work with the Afar and reports on the atrocities within Djibouti.

I mailed them off to aid agencies, and trudged around Addis Ababa delivering them by hand to the US, Canadian and European Union embassies. Australia didn't have an embassy in Addis, so I posted a copy to the one in Nairobi, in Kenya, which had responsibility for Ethiopia.

Whenever possible, I tried to deliver my update to the first secretary in person. I'd turn up at the embassy gate with my shoulder sack of roneoed sheets, looking like a newsboy, and ask for an interview. I think I must have livened up their rather dull lives, for, as often as not, they invited me for morning tea. I found it ironic that we'd sit around sipping tea from exquisite china cups, accompanied by little delicacies flown in from their home countries, discussing food shortages in Djibouti.

'How dreadful. Starving, you say. Here, have another biscuit, they're from Fortnum & Mason.'

My favourite host was the first secretary of the German embassy, Count von Kitlitz. He was some kind of aristocrat, I believe, but he had a good heart. Once he gave me a consignment of high-protein biscuits for the civilians who were cut off in the north. He admonished me not to tell anyone it was German food. 'I don't care about regulations. You've got camels, take the damn stuff, don't let these people starve.'

Eventually, the aid agencies started to take an interest. Someone from Oxfam Great Britain called one day and said, 'Thanks for the little information sheet. Why don't you come in and we'll have a chat?'

My old friends from the Eritrea and Tigray campaigns, Community Aid Abroad, in Australia, contributed some funds; then my brother George used his influence with AngliCORD, the aid arm of the Melbourne Anglican Diocese. Bit by bit, funds trickled in. When we still found ourselves short, we'd dip into my money in the Djibouti bank.

Count von Kitlitz had introduced me to his gorgeous wife, and one day we received a gold-embossed invitation card asking us to attend a cocktail party at the embassy. Our Afar friends thought this was a great joke. We didn't own any decent clothing, so they took it upon themselves to find suitable outfits. After many telephone calls, they assembled shoes, a shirt, pants and a jacket for Ismael. There was great hilarity when he had to tie his tie, having never done such a thing in his life.

Someone lent me a beautiful and expensive Afar dress, and also some high heels, but when I tried to walk in them I found I was on the verge of toppling over all the time. I couldn't risk falling flat on my face at the embassy, so I went with some reasonably presentable flatties instead.

We thought it would never do to arrive on foot, but we had no money for a taxi. Our friends took care of that too, raising enough for the trip both there and back.

The reception was held in the ambassador's residence adjacent to the embassy. After cocktails, we were shown into a formal dining room where there was a long table laden with cutlery. Ismael and I were seated quite a distance away from each other. He looked in dismay at the utensils lined up beside his plate. We were too far apart to talk to one another, so he signalled his confusion to me with furtive gestures.

I'd been using my hands to eat for so long I couldn't remember if you were meant to start on the outside or the inside. In the end, we both waited to see what the others did and copied them.

We hadn't realised that we were the guests of honour and therefore each had to make a speech. When the meal finished, the ambassador tapped his glass and introduced Ismael. He got to his feet and made what I thought was a pretty good speech about what we were doing to help the Afar. He ended, 'And now my wife, Valerie, would like to add a few words.'

I managed to blurt out something. It seemed to go over all right because they all applauded, and later several of them milled around wanting to know more.

The embassy reception was a strange, almost surreal experience – as foreign to us as a trip to Mars. When it was over, we went home in our finery to the refugees on the floor, the shared bathroom, the peeling paint, the cockroaches, the camp-cooker, and Aisha – happy to be back once more in the real world.

The Browning children (left to right): Nick, George, Valerie, Pauline, David, Jacqueline and Rosemary. This picture was taken just before Carolyn's birth, late in 1953.

Graduation day at nursing school, 1971.

Party time with a Somali friend in Saudi Arabia.

With Mother and Father at our wedding reception, minus the groom.

With newly born Aisha in the Djibouti flat.

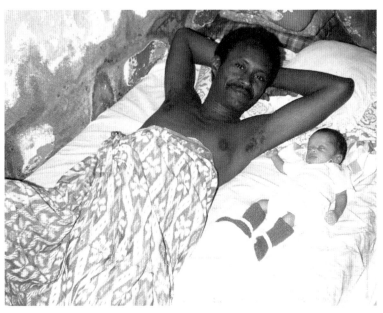

The proud father with his daughter.

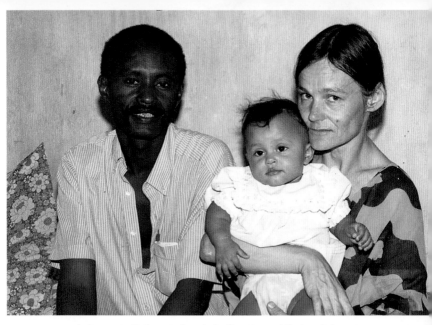

At home in Djibouti shortly before Ismael fled to Ethiopia.

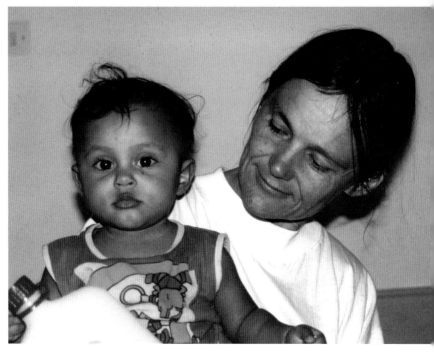

With Aisha, aged about one.

My kitchen in Shola Makananya, Addis Ababa.

Aisha, aged seven.

Rammidos.

A happy family portrait.

Ismael's 'office' in Logia in a corner of the meeting room.

ANNA LITTLE

Enid Parker with her Afar/English dictionary.

Drinking camel's milk from a woven-palm-leaf bowl.

A classic Afar face.
The necklace pouches
contain Koranic verses.

Afar girls wearing typical jewellery.

An Afar beauty with a
traditional hairstyle.

A life-giving pause.

Moving house.

A typical *deboita*.

Lecturing young men about the dangers of smoking.

Teaching women health workers.

With health workers on a vaccination trip.

APDA health worker giving out vaccinations.

Conferring with Haalima, the extension worker, about problems in the Gewwaane area.

Approaching a village to follow up reports of childhood malnutrition.

Checking a baby for malnutrition. The mother in the
background has malaria.

Valerie and Haalima examine a malnourished child.

An APDA-trained teacher gives a lesson to nomad students.

Learning to read and write in Afar.

Valerie and Ismael in Australia.

CHAPTER 12

Towards the end of 1994, we made plans for the three of us to go to Australia so that my family could meet Ismael and Aisha. When we went to immigration to obtain clearances to leave the country, there was big trouble. I had no entry stamp in my passport. When I'd come in from Djibouti two years earlier, I had been a little flustered. I had Aisha cradled in one arm, and I was lugging a couple of plastic bags full of bits and pieces with the other. I was worried that the old *persona non grata* edict might still come back to cause me trouble. With my small stature, my eyes barely reached the level of the immigration counter, so I couldn't really see what the officer was doing. After all this time, I now discovered that he had forgotten to stamp my passport. In my anxiety to get the whole business over with, I hadn't bothered to check. I had been living in Ethiopia illegally.

When I worked out what had happened, I tried to explain it to the official who was interviewing us. He was having none of it. I ended up having to go to court to defend a charge of illegal entry. We couldn't afford a lawyer, so I represented myself, with Ismael translating from the Amharic for me. The judge listened carefully while I explained the oversight. Then he advised me that if I wished to make that the grounds for my defence, the case would take a long time, as they'd have to check back through the airport records. His advice was to plead guilty and pay a fine.

We could have been waiting for months before we could leave to go to Australia. We reluctantly agreed to pay the fine and waited anxiously to see how much it would be. The judge looked me up and down, and conferred with the prosecutor. Ismael told me later what he'd said. 'Look at her, she's obviously been living in the bush, she hasn't even got proper shoes, she's only got those plastic things. These are obviously very poor people. We'll give them a low fine.'

He fined me 300 birr, about A\$40, and told us we were free to leave.

That wasn't the end of our difficulties, however. Ismael had already filed his visa application with the Australian Embassy in Nairobi. We'd filled in all the forms and sent them off by registered post, as we couldn't afford a courier. Weeks went by without any word. I had a distressing telephone conversation with my father where, in the midst of a general harangue, he asked, 'Do you want me to die before I see my son-in-law and my granddaughter?'

'Of course not, Father. I never wanted to do this to you, it's not my idea, it's the embassy.'

He went on and on. I was a thoughtless woman, I did not care about my family. I was being callous towards him, and so on and so on. It was like revisiting my childhood. When he hung up, I was in tears.

After a lot of long-distance pestering, the embassy informed us that they'd lost our application. We then sent a second one, filling out all the forms once more, sending new photographs, plus the money for the visa. This time we sent it by courier.

We were informed by the company that it had arrived. More time went by without a reply. I called the embassy to check that they had a record of the package arriving. The desk person told me they'd received it and he gave me a receipt number, but still no one could find any trace of our application.

My brother George knew lots of influential people in Canberra. In despair, I scraped together some money to ring him and ask for his help. George had a quiet drink with someone he knew in the Department of Immigration. There was an investigation, which revealed that a clerk in the embassy had sold our documents. The culprit was dismissed. The embassy sent new documents to us via courier and told us to return them at their expense. From then on things moved swiftly. Our papers arrived and at last we were able to leave.

Aisha and Ismael were big hits in Australia. My husband and my mother formed an instant bond. What impressed Ismael was her concern for each member of the family. He'd seen how, without fail, every fifteen days I'd get a letter from her. I could count the days by their arrival. She'd write summaries of all my brothers' and sisters' news, plus that of their children and their children's children. She was always urging me to keep in touch with them. She was a tremendous matriarchal figure. Father didn't approve of what I was doing in Ethiopia but my mother was always supportive. If I was feeling low she'd write: 'Don't think too much of the toughness, think of the future, think of what's happening to the people.' My father was the family disciplinarian, but my mother held us together with love.

Ever after their first meeting, Ismael called her his 'heart mother'. He didn't know when his birthday was, so Mother decided it was in January. Every January, she would send him a shirt. They remained close until the day she died.

We spent time with all my brothers and sisters. Ismael got on especially well with George, who by then was Bishop of

Canberra. The first time they met, they had a long discussion about religion. Ismael wanted to know how Christianity had changed from its simple origins to having today's grandiose churches with priests dressed in finery while the poor remained as poor as ever. George and Ismael were together in the yard cooking a barbecue while Margaret and I were in the kitchen preparing salads. They got so involved that they quite forgot the time. When they finally came inside with a plate of very cool steaks, George apologised for keeping us waiting so long. My brother enjoyed their discussions immensely.

Even Father was accepting, in his own inhibited way. His sense of duty came to the fore. It was as if he were thinking that now he had a son-in-law, he needed to behave like a father-in-law towards him. It had taken four years for Father to meet Ismeal, so he'd had a long time to get used to the idea. Even if he didn't approve, he couldn't do anything about it, as he certainly didn't believe in divorce.

Father had always been a distant man who found it hard to form relationships. I think he regarded Ismael as a member of some sort of exotic species which had somehow fetched up in his living room. Ismael would never have been able to have a heart-to-heart talk with him as he could with Mother or my brothers. Nevertheless, Father was generously welcoming and he tried hard to make Ismael's stay as easy as possible.

When we left Australia we flew to Bangkok intending to connect with an Ethiopian Airlines flight to Addis Ababa. The plane was late leaving, so we missed our connection. We soon found that there were no other flights to be had. Everything heading in our direction was booked solid for days ahead. Our only hope seemed to be if there was a cancellation.

We spent the next three days in the airport. In between visiting airline counters, we wandered around pushing our trolley, looking in shops and trying to keep Aisha amused. We slept on the airport seats and washed up in the public toilets. Through a combination of stress and boredom, I nearly went crazy.

In the end, the best we could find was a flight to Athens. It wasn't Ethiopia, it wasn't even Africa, but it was heading roughly in the right direction.

When we arrived in Athens, Ismael said he wanted to contact the Ethiopian embassy. I couldn't see much point but he said he was sick of being in foreign countries, he just wanted to speak to an Ethiopian. It was just as well that he did. He found out that, while we'd been away, the immigration laws had changed. I now needed a re-entry visa. If I arrived without it, they'd deport me back to Australia.

The man at the embassy was sympathetic. After hearing what we'd been through for the last few days, he said, 'Let me try and help.' He gave me the visa, and – more good luck – there was a flight available to Addis Ababa.

When we flew back and settled in at home, there was more trouble with the authorities. They said that, even though I was married to Ismael, I couldn't stay. Ismael was okay because he was an Afar, but for some bureaucratic reason his wife could not be in Ethiopia unless he could prove that he had a job. You could hardly call what he did a job, and it was totally illegal anyway. He was told he'd have to register as a businessman. This he did, calling himself an importer/exporter. After that, they told me it was all right, I could stay.

Even then we were on shaky ground. The state security police were suspicious of what we were up to. An Afar liberation movement, Uguguma, was engaged in sporadic guerilla warfare with government soldiers in the north. Their aim was to achieve proper recognition by the Ethiopian government of the Afar region. The fact that I disappeared into the bush now and then made the police suspect I could be running guns to the guerillas.

The people at the Taitu Hotel had told us that our phone had been tapped, and we kept hearing odd clicking noises whenever we made calls from our house in Addis. Whenever we were in the capital we were followed. I became used to seeing familiar gentlemen in civilian clothing sitting behind me in tea houses, or following me at a not-so-discreet distance to and from meetings. Ismael and I lived in a state of constant insecurity, never knowing if we were going to be arrested.

After the first few trips I had stopped taking Aisha with me into Djibouti. She was old enough to stay behind and be looked after by either Ismael, or our house girl if Ismael was busy somewhere else. In late 1994 I was on a trip inside Djibouti. We had just made camp for the night at an Afar settlement when a young man named Korbo came running to me in a state of great agitation.

'Have you heard what's happened? It's so exciting. Ugure Kefli has made an arrangement with the government. We're all going back in.'

Ugure Kefli was the FRUD military leader. I said, 'What do you mean, we're all going back in?'

'They're going to allow the Afar to share the government. Isn't it wonderful? Your husband could be a minister, he could be something.'

I felt as if someone had punched me in the guts. We'd been betrayed. Under pressure from France, the president, Hassan Gouled Aptidon, had agreed to rearrange his cabinet so some FRUD people could be included. This was far short of equality, and a sell-out of all that we had been fighting for. I said to

Korbo, 'Please don't speak about this to Ismael. He'll go crazy, he'll hit himself, he'll hurt himself – don't speak about this.'

'No, your white brain doesn't understand. It's going to be really good, and we'll be part of it.'

Ismael was with Aisha in Eli Daar in Ethiopia; I had to get back to him as soon as possible. The camels had never seemed to move so slowly. I begrudged each minute we spent stopped for food or sleep. We crossed the border without incident and made our way into Eli Daar. Aisha gave me her usual big hug of welcome. I could tell immediately that Ismael had still not heard the news. He was his normal, cheerful self. After we'd chatted for a while about the trip, he said, 'Get in the truck, we're off to a meeting.'

'It's not good, Ismael,' I said.

'What's not good?'

I was too frightened to tell him what I knew. All I could do was repeat, 'I know it's not going to be good.'

'Nonsense. You don't know anything about our discussions. Everything's okay.'

The meeting was in Assaita. When we got there, the leaders were all waiting for us with smiles on their faces.

'What's the topic?' said Ismael.

'Good news, Ismael, tomorrow we're going to Yoboki [just inside the border in Djibouti]. There'll be army trucks coming to meet us and take us to Djibouti City.'

'What? What are you talking about?'

'We're going in, Ismael. It's over. We're going to have a place in the government.'

Ismael's face turned to stone. He grabbed me by my dress and pulled me to the door. 'Get out of here, woman.'

I started to say something, but he interrupted me. 'Don't speak, there's nothing to say.'

I scooped Aisha up into my arms and left. This was not something that would involve women.

The meeting went on until midnight. When Ismael came out, he did not speak. He didn't need to. I could tell that he'd lost. Three years of struggle, and countless lost and broken lives, had been for nothing. His comrades had sold out for the promise of the comfortable job, the nice Toyota and a cushy life.

With Aisha and me in tow, Ismael strode into the street and accosted some poor fellow with a broken-down Toyota HiLux. He demanded that he drive us to Logia, 65 kilometres away. The man protested that his car wasn't up to it. Ismael insisted, 'I don't care if it breaks down, drive us now.'

During the entire trip to Logia, Ismael did not utter a word. It was nearly two in the morning when we arrived. He thrust some money at the driver, then strode along the lines of parked trucks until he found one that was going to Eli Daar, 150 kilometres away. Our journey finally ended at dawn. And, at last, Ismael said, 'Yes, now I can speak to you.'

He was crushed. The Afar martyrs hadn't suffered and died so that these people could end up in a government still subservient to the Issa. Some of those young idealists who had slept on our floor in Djibouti, and who had been so passionate about Afar rights, are now cabinet ministers. No more sleeping on floors for them, no more running from the Issa army; they are living a life of privilege. But for the Afar community in Djibouti, little has changed.

Our former comrades did not take kindly to being rejected. In the middle of the night, sometimes at two or three in the morning, the telephone would ring. If I answered, a voice would say that they were going to come and kill me and brutalise my family. If Ismael answered, they'd try to turn him against me, telling him that I was a western women's liberationist trying to change the Afar. They'd say that I didn't have any respect for marriage and that one day I'd ditch him. They'd suggest that I might have had Aisha by another man. How did Ismael know he was the father?

After these phone calls, Ismael would pace the house in a state of great distress. I thought he'd go mad. If someone insults me, I just explode and tell them what I think of them but Ismael internalises everything. He'd always suffered from gastritis. The symptoms are a burning pain in the stomach, and the attacks can be extremely debilitating. I'm sure it was because of this persecution that he began to have such severe attacks that at times he couldn't get up. His bouts of sciatica continued too. Sometimes they were so severe that he was unable to walk.

Whilst all this was going on, the Ethiopian government continued to harass us. Once the border police came to us where we were staying in Bure and demanded that we come to their office for an interview. They accused us straight out of sending medicine across the border.

Ismael told them, 'I don't care about borders. Eritrea and Djibouti and Ethiopia are all Afar. It's none of your business. If you have evidence, show me. If not, then you can catch me at the border.'

'What is your business in Djibouti?'

'That's nothing to do with you. I'm working for my people. You have to take care of the borders, not ask me my business.'

I think Ismael would have made a good lawyer. In the end, they let us go and, needless to say, they never did catch us crossing the border.

Sometimes the attempts to incriminate us were more subtle. Two people from the UN came to see us in Assaita and asked us to take them into the Danakil Depression. They wanted to write a report about Uguguma. The rebels were based in very harsh country near Lake Afdera. The UN people had received permission from the regional government to enter and been given two four-wheel drives and a government minder. Allegedly, we were asked to go because we knew the country.

There was a road for the first part of the trip; after that, they'd have to hire camels. The plan was for us to leave them, take the cars to Mekele and pick them up again.

We discovered later that the government never had any intention of allowing the UN to meet with Uguguma. The camel owner whom they found for them asked 500 birr for one camel for one day – a ridiculous sum. Not surprisingly, the UN people refused to pay, and we all drove back to Assaita.

The government minder told Ismael later that if we'd come back without the UN people, we'd have been charged with aiding the rebels and sent to prison. It had been his job to prevent the meeting; it was lucky for us that he succeeded. Such are the devious ways of African politics.

In 1996 we were called in to the government offices and threatened with criminal charges and/or deportation unless we legalised our organisation. After the changes in Djibouti, we'd been turning our attention more to the needs of Afar within Ethiopia. It seemed appropriate to change our name from the Djibouti Relief Association and to register ourselves officially as the Afar Relief Association. This would later become the Afar Pastoral Development Association (APDA), the name under which we operate today.

We still lived in a state of insecurity. Twice the Ministry of the Interior threatened to deport me. There was a lot of unrest in the Afar region and everyone was suspicious of everyone else. Being married to Ismael and having Aisha made no difference. They said I could just leave the child behind. The regional government mistrusted us just as much. On three different occasions when I was in the Afar region, friends advised me to disappear for a while, as the authorities wanted to arrest me.

It reached the point where I had to do something. The tension and insecurity were ruining our family life. Ismael's health was suffering, I couldn't see a future for Aisha, I was always wondering if I'd be thrown into prison. It had got to the point where I was wondering which sister would be best suited to look after Aisha when it happened, as I thought that Mother would probably be too old.

Years before in Sudan, I'd known a Tigrinya man, Hagos Araya; I used to see him all the time in the tea shops of Khartoum. He went on to become a big man in the EPLF. Then, when the TPLF joined them in the fight against Ethiopia, he'd been seconded to them. Hagos was now the Ethiopian Prime Minister's closest adviser. I telephoned him from a public phone, wondering if he'd still remember me.

'I remember you well,' he said. 'I've been expecting you for years to come and visit me.'

I made an appointment for a couple of days away. Walking back to the house I wondered if I'd done the right thing. By confronting the government I might make matters worse, not better. I worried, too, about the effect it would have on Ismael.

When I got home, I told him what I'd done. 'I've been thinking that I've caused you enough trouble, and it seems that life isn't going well, so let me sort it out with the government. Let them make a decision, for Aisha's sake. And if it has to be, let me do the prison time or otherwise let's see some solution. I'll give them our banking details and ask them to do a total evaluation, let them look at all our records and then say whether or not I'm fit to stay in Ethiopia.'

Ismael asked me, 'What do you know about this Hagos Araya?'

'He's a political man in the TPLF. Eritrean by birth, but close to the Prime Minister.'

'Does he speak Tigrinya?'

'Of course, he was born in that area.'

'Then I'm going too.'

'Do you really think so? I don't want to make you more nervous.'

Ismael was adamant that he wanted to be included in the discussion. I made another call and asked if I could bring my husband with me.

Hagos agreed, adding, 'Don't bring the child. I'm telling you, I know all about you, so when you're in my office don't waste my time with this and that chatter about family. I know all your business, I have everything. It's all on file.'

'I'm sure you do,' I said, thinking of the surveillance and the phone taps. I was confident that they couldn't have found anything too incriminating. At the Taitu Hotel, a minder had once said to Ismael, 'Your wife's so boring. I've been looking after this case for so long I'm going to tell my boss to take me off it. She never does anything interesting.'

A couple of days later we were shown into a plain government office. 'Hello, Hagos,' I said. 'It's been a long time. We've known each other for years.'

'Yes, but you've never come to see me.'

'Because you're in a government position. It's my belief that we haven't been treated correctly. We're a family. I have a child.'

'I know that, don't talk about that.'

'I want to try and calm down and live a somewhat normal life. I don't want to be always running and fearing something. I want to be straight with you and straight with the government.'

With Ismael translating, I put my proposal to him. 'All right,' said Hagos. 'We'll evaluate your organisation. If what you claim you do, health and such, is correct, then you'll be okay. If it's all a big blown-up lie, you'll get it.'

We had a couple of visits from investigators, who went through our records. Surprisingly, they asked us very few questions. A report was written and a copy given to us. As it was in Amharic, I've never been able to read it, but apparently it was very favourable. From then on, there were no more phone taps, no more surveillance.

CHAPTER 13

In the early days there were no statistics at all about health in the Afar region. Not that we needed statistics to be aware that the situation was dire. I only had to sit for a while with the women in any encampment and hear their stories, to know that practically every family had suffered loss through illness or childbirth. In 1997, APDA carried out the first-ever survey of health in distant rural areas. The result gave us a shock. We found that the under-five-year-old mortality rate was about 35 per cent! We could not get sufficient data to estimate the maternal death rate. As an indication, though, in 2006 it was 1.39 per 1000, which is almost twelve times the Ethiopian national average.

Living far from any hospitals or health clinics, it was unheard-of for nomadic women to have proper antenatal care. The danger of childbirth is compounded by several harmful traditional practices. For instance, women in labour aren't given food or drink. The Afar believe that the uterus and bladder are connected and the swallowed liquid will enter the uterus and cause bleeding.

Most women wait for some time before starting breast-feeding. This ranges from a few hours to five nights. In the meantime, the newly born infant is fed on goat's milk and butter.

The mother and baby are washed after the birth, and after that, neither mother nor baby is washed for seven days. Instead, they smoke the *deboita*. A smoky fire is lit inside and the mats pulled down to cover the entrance. Mother and baby remain inside while the smoking takes place.

A major cause of maternal death is retained placenta. Also, it's common to bleed the mother extensively before the placenta is delivered to get rid of 'bad blood'.

Many mothers are far too young to be having babies. They've often been married at fifteen, some as young as thirteen or fourteen. We found a few instances of girls being married before they had even begun menstruating. Often, their little bodies are simply not ready for childbirth.

Female genital mutilation is also a factor. Usually, an assistant will cut the vagina before birth, but we came across cases where the woman had had no one to help and had had to try to force the baby out through an opening the size of a pencil, with severe damage as a result. One woman had resorted to cutting herself to give birth. After a child has been born, women are sewn up again or the wound may be held together with thorns.

In 1997 there were two hospitals with a total of about 70 beds to serve more than a million people spread over an area larger than Victoria. There were a few clinics and health centres, but these were of no use to people who spent their lives far away from them in the desert.

In addition to the expected diseases and occasional epidemics, we found that there was a lot of anaemia. The Afar live mainly on milk and bread, and don't realise that this diet has no iron content. I remember once visiting a man whose wife was pregnant. He'd called me into his *deboita* because she was too weak to get up. Every time she tried to stand she felt giddy.

It was obvious that she was anaemic. I told him this and explained about low red cell counts. He said to me, 'I don't understand. I know she's pregnant, so I've deliberately allotted goats for her milk.'

'There's no iron in milk,' I said.

'Of course there is.'

'No. It's good for the bones and the teeth, and good for growing children because it's got protein in it, but it doesn't help the blood, and you need iron in your blood.'

'This is news. So what should my wife eat?'

'Well, you can't kill meat every day, I know that. You should try and buy lentils and boil them, or get *shiro*. You'll have to do something special for her.'

He said, 'I'll do it, where do I get this stuff?'

'Just go to town and ask for it in the shop and they'll sell it to you by the kilo.'

'That's not a problem,' he replied. 'I'll take some goats to town and sell them.'

This was a classic case of lack of education. He and his wife just did what the Afar had been doing since time immemorial. Modern health education had never reached them out in the desert.

While training health workers we had to overcome many misconceptions. For instance, the Afar believe there is good and bad blood. It's difficult for them to understand what the nervous system is, or enzymes, or hormones, or white and red blood cells. There are no words in Afar for these things, so we had to create words for them.

Ismael and I knew that the government's conventional approach to health care would never work for the Afar. Fixed buildings are useless for a nomadic society. So, instead of Afar coming to where the care was, the care would have to come to them.

We developed a system where the community itself selects someone to be a health worker. If there's no one with formal education, non-literate people can be chosen, then the first thing we do is teach them to read and write. The important thing is that they're highly motivated to help their community.

The health worker receives six months' training. This includes the government's curriculum for community health workers, as well as a special course on diagnosing common illnesses in remote communities. They're given a 200-page illustrated training manual which is written in Afar. After the initial training, they serve another six months in the field to fulfil the practical part of the course. Each health worker is given annual refresher courses.

The workers travel with the community as they move from water source to water source in search of fresh pasture for their herds. Each worker must visit each household at least once a month. This frequently involves walking long distances, as the communities are often widely scattered.

For people to learn about good health practices, they need to be literate. Very early on, our health workers were reporting that it was hard to get people to change their lifestyle, and do such basic things as use soap, or wash their babies regularly. Without literacy, it's as if you're trapped in a box and can't see out. You're aware of your history, so you do things because that's the way they've always been done. To break open that box, which is fixed and rigid, you need to be able to use your brain. When you can read and write, your brain becomes new. You become excited by education and learning, and you change.

The government estimated that only 2 per cent of Afar could

read and write. Ismael and I decided that we'd start a literacy program. Afar had only very recently become a written language, thanks to the work of the Red Sea Mission Team and, in particular, one of their members, the English missionary Dr Enid Parker. I'd briefly met Enid whilst I was living in Djibouti. Hers was a remarkable story.

Her first encounter with the Afar had been in 1957, when she went as a missionary to Thio on the Red Sea coast, and opened a school. Thio was in the Afar region of Eritrea, then part of Ethiopia. At that time, the language was not written down, so, in order to progress with education, people had to learn another language – usually French in Djibouti, and Amharic in Ethiopia and Eritrea.

The founder of the Red Sea Mission Team, Dr Lionel Gurney, had brought a linguist from America to work on the Afar language. He'd married one of the missionary nurses, who contracted encephalitis, so they had to be sent home. Dr Gurney then asked Enid to take over the work. She told him that she couldn't, as she had no training. As there was no one else, Dr Gurney sent Enid to do a course at the Summer Institute of Linguistics (SIL) at Wycliffe Bible Translators, in Buckinghamshire, England. Students at SIL were taught every sound that it's possible to make with the human voice and how to write it down phonetically. They learnt how to look at a piece of language to determine where the verb was, what the parts of speech were and how the grammar worked.

Until then, Red Sea Mission Team members had simply been writing down what they heard. You can pick up common expressions pretty quickly. You write them down, then start to make 'frame sentences'. For example: Where have you come from? I came from the well; I came from the village; I came from the mountains; I came from my house.

When they had a sentence and some different nouns, they'd

turn the sentence around: Where has he come from? Where has she come from? Where have they come from?

In this way the team could find out what the nouns and pronouns were, how the verbs went, and eventually build up the language.

The first thing Enid translated into written form was John's Gospel. She then set about writing primers for the Afar people to learn to read and write their own language. She asked for SIL help. The people at SIL requested she bring tape recordings of Afar conversing and telling stories. She spent time with a linguist who'd been working in Papua New Guinea, and together they worked out how to create the primers.

Not every language is learnt in the same way. They decided very quickly that the best method to teach Afar would be the Syllable Method, whereby students learned the syllables constituting a word, rather than initially learning individual letters. As soon as possible, the learned words were used in short sentences. This was combined with the Look and Say method, where for long words the student would just look at the word and remember what it was, rather than breaking it up into syllables.

The Latin script was chosen, firstly to make it easier for Enid and also because it would enable the language to be typewritten easily. In the early 1970s, the Afar President of Djibouti, Ali Aref Bourhan, confirmed the choice.

The Afar have three sounds that we don't have in English: a retroflex 'd', made by curling the tongue to the roof of the mouth; a guttural 'khhh'; and 'ain', as in Arabic, which is a restriction of the throat. There are seven letters in our alphabet which the Afar do not use, so there were seven to choose from to represent these sounds. The Afar chose 'x' for the retroflex 'd', for 'khhh' they chose 'c', and for 'ain' they chose 'q'. Double letters indicate long vowel sounds. There is wide use of double consonants too, which are simply written twice.

By 1972, Enid had produced five primers. Language lessons were prepared and an Afar man was trained to teach them. He recorded the lessons on tape so students could listen with the primer in front of them.

In 1969 a missionary colleague of Enid's, Margaret Munro, had started a school for girls in Thio. This, by the way, was quite a radical thing to do in those days. Before, only boys had gone to school; the women didn't leave the house in daytime. Margaret told the clan leader, 'You're educating the boys and when they become educated, they don't want donkeys for wives. It's important you educate the little girls.'

The leader had agreed, and they'd begun with about twenty girls. When Margaret went home to England on leave, she checked their progress with a primary school specialist. The results were astonishing. Using Enid's methods, they'd covered about four years' work in two years.

Enid then went to Djibouti, where she trialled her primers on three completely uneducated boys. They had to attend lessons every day for an hour, for three months, with the usual days off. At the end of the three months, they could read and write their own language.

Dr Enid Parker has devoted her life to Afar literacy. She went on to produce an English/Afar/French dictionary which was published in 1985 and reprinted in 1992. It had 8000 entries, each comprising an Afar word, a part of speech, an English translation and a French translation. While this was very useful, Enid and her co-author, Professor Richard Hayward, realised that it would have been preferable to include example sentences to illustrate the intent of a word more fully than a single-word translation did.

She then began work on an English/Afar dictionary which

would take 21 years to complete. It finally included 13,500 English words with their Afar translations, and, amazingly, an example sentence for every one.

This mammoth work was completed and published in 2006, by an American publisher, Dunwoody Press, which specialises in 'less taught' languages. As I write this, Enid, who's now 86, is visiting Addis Ababa from her home in England. She's as energetic and fit as ever, leading a busy social life as she catches up with old friends. She's attending meetings all over town while seeking a local publisher to make the dictionary available cheaply in the Afar region.

We knew of Enid Parker's five primer books, but we wanted a system under which to use them. We heard that UNESCO was looking for people to pilot an 'emergency teacher's package' in Afar. They'd tried it in Angola, Rwanda and Somalia with success. We were the fourth.

In the course of a series of meetings, we worked out an Afar teaching manual and put together a resources kit that was entirely portable. It consisted of school supplies for 80 children, including slates, exercise books, HB pencils, erasers, chalk, cloth dusters and an attendance register.

For the teacher, there was black paint for a blackboard, a paintbrush, a blackboard duster, four ball-point pens, four black fine markers, twenty HB pencils, five pencil sharpeners, a note book, a box of white chalk, a box of coloured chalk, three printed cloth charts of the alphabet, numbers and multiplication tables and 10 Scrabble sets in cloth drawstring bags.

In early 1996 UNESCO sent us an education expert from the Netherlands to teach us how to use these resources. Ismael and I were in the first training workshop in Andabba when in burst two elderly Afar clan leaders demanding to be included. They were classic Afar desert men, swarthy and wrinkled, with dusty blankets over their shoulders and carrying rifles. I was worried about what the UNESCO woman would think. I said to Ismael, 'These old men are going to break up the meeting. What can I do?'

'Get rid of them.'

I said, 'I can't, you'll have to talk to them.'

'I can't leave, I have to stay here. I'm the translator.'

So I said to them, 'Come with me, my uncles, I have an issue with you. Let's sit under the tree outside and discuss. You will be very disappointed if you get in that meeting. It's not what you want. I know what you want. You want treatment for malaria and health things. This is not health, this is education.'

They said, 'Don't insult us. You think we don't want education, is that what you are thinking? You are not right. We send our camel caravan from Afar all the way into Tigray. They go as far as Mekele to get the things we need. When the men come back, we ask them what they have seen with their eyes and what they have heard with their ears. They tell us that the Tigrayans are meeting, they're doing, they're building, they're changing their lives. They tell us fantastic stories. We wonder about ourselves. We are sleeping under trees. The Afar are going nowhere. We have no future and you are trying to stop us being involved in education? How dare you. By clan law, you could be punished for doing this. You are insulting us.'

I was shocked. I had misjudged them completely. I'd thought they would be resistant to education; instead, they were demanding it. I said, 'Listen, my uncles, I'm just trying to help you. But you must know if you are to be involved, we will want to involve females as students.'

'This is not a problem,' one replied. 'I am a clan elder. If I tell the women to attend class, they will attend class.'

These two old men had come all the way from Mille, each

with one of their sons, a distance of 300 kilometres. They demanded that we admit the boys to the training. We were happy to agree.

This was the first time I really understood that the Afar were desperate for a future where they would be empowered to do things for themselves.

The workshops went on for seven days. In April, the literacy program began with 21 boys who'd already had a little bit of education. After training, we sent them out into the communities. This wasn't entirely successful. They were town boys and they couldn't put up with the harsh life of the nomads. And, as they weren't from those communities, they didn't have the motivation to stick it out.

Our approach now is the same as with health workers. The clan selects the candidates, most often people who have a high reputation in the community. Using Enid's primers, we teach them how to read and write in about two months. Once they have acquired literacy, they're given another two months' training which introduces them to such things as the principles and methods of teaching (pedagogy), teaching resources, and how to report their activities. This equips them with the skills to teach literacy in their first service year. They're then sent back to the community with the portable teaching kit, which can be packed up and carried in a backpack or on a camel.

After they've taught for a year, they're given two months of training to upgrade their skills. They have further upgrading every July during the hot season. A person from the Bureau of Education monitors the training and teaches them Amharic. APDA has five other trainers for the additional subjects, including pedagogy, Afar grammar, mathematics, environmental science and English.

It has taken a long time for the government to approve our methods. At first, they considered that a candidate for teaching had to be functionally literate – that is, they had to have at least completed Grade Six. They'd put teachers through a training course and send them out to the community. The trouble was that they didn't stay. The government now recognises that teaching without all of the usual infrastructure can work.

From the government's point of view, this is all pioneering stuff, but what we're doing is really nothing new to the pastoralists. They've long had itinerant *Koranic* teachers who moved with the community. When we train a teacher, he or she goes back into the community highly motivated to see their people improve. APDA asks the community to help the teachers and health workers by transporting their materials by camel, supplying stones and wood towards the construction of a simple shelter for teaching and to contribute a goat per household to APDA.

Soon after our program began, I was inside a *deboita*, attending to a sick woman. A group of other Afar stood about outside waiting to see me. A young boy pushed his way inside in front of everyone else. I blew my top, shouting to him to get to the end of the queue.

He probably wasn't used to being spoken to like that by a woman. He answered back, and we started to have a bit of a spat. I said to him, 'Wait your turn. I can see that you're not so sick.'

'I didn't come here for treatment,' he said.

'Well, get out of here.'

He glared at me, then threw an exercise book through the door. 'Read it.'

He'd written on the front and back cover, on both sides of every page, in the margins – every spare space was covered with writing.

'What on earth is this?' I said.

'I've just finished learning to read and write, and I'm writing our family history.'

I looked more closely. It was true. He'd put down their history going back through generations: how they came to this area, what sort of people they were, their relationship with the camel herders . . . all of the oral history which had been handed down by his father and grandfather, recorded faithfully onto the page. He'd run out of paper and wanted me to give him another exercise book, and he was so excited that he couldn't wait.

Ismael and I had never doubted our vision but this keen young boy was living proof that the literacy program was working. We now have 236 teachers in the field, reaching about 27 per cent of the Afar pastoral society, with support from some fifteen international NGOs and agencies.

CHAPTER 14

Over time, we've refined the health program. We realised that a lot of our work involved helping women, yet we had no women working in health except me. In 1999 we taught our first class of 36 pastoral women how to read and write. From these we chose the best twenty to be 'extension workers'. Their job description is somewhere between that of a health worker and a teacher. They're basically awareness-raisers. They tell women about disease, hygiene, sanitation, improved birthing practices and so on, but they don't handle medicines or treat patients.

The extension workers encourage women towards education. Another of their tasks is to train the traditional birth attendants (TBAs), who are already living in the communities. They teach them how to conduct antenatal and postnatal checking and which pregnancies to refer to the hospital when a home delivery will be risky. The TBAs are provided with a 'clean delivery set' consisting of cotton wool, cord ties, a bandage for the cord stump, cloth to wipe and wrap the baby, plastic gloves to protect the TBA from blood, a new razor blade, and a plastic sheet to put under the mother.

TBAs were usually the women in the community who

specialised in circumcising young girls. With APDA's guidance, they are now at the forefront of our campaign against female genital mutilation. It's thought the practice originated in Pharaonic times in Egypt, since evidence of female circumcision has been found in mummies. Some scholars say that there are links between the Afar and the Pharaohs. It's believed that the substance used to mummify bodies comes from trees found in the Mabla area of northern Djibouti. There are words and names from hieroglyphs in the Afar language; Afar mark their camels with hieroglyphic letters, and there are hieroglyphic paintings in Afar rock art.

Afar traditional dress shows Pharaonic influences. Young men cut their hair straight across the forehead and wear it long at the sides and back, similar to the style seen on wall paintings in ancient Egyptian ruins. The female hairstyle of long plaits coming to the centre of the forehead, called *beseeta*; a bride's decoration and head cloth; the man's traditional garb of a simple sarong and bare chest, all seem to support the link.

In Afar society all children are circumcised – male and female. For males it's purely a traditional rite of passage, under-taken from when they are seven to fifteen years old. Before the operation takes place, the boys are shaved. They tie a red ribbon around their forehead and are given a traditional curved knife. As the operation begins, the circumciser attempts to distract his patient by asking him to speak the names of all the cattle his relatives possess. The hapless lad continues to shout out the names while the painful removal of the foreskin takes place. The ceremony usually involves a group of boys having the procedure. The boys stay together for about two weeks until they recover from their wounds. From that time on, they are considered to be fully-fledged men, initiated into clan membership and subject to all the clan obligations and laws. They are allowed to wear a knife and have a rifle, curl their hair and get married.

For girls, circumcision is done so that they will retain their virginity until marriage. The operation is performed when they are very young. Using a razor blade, or a knife, the labia majora and clitoris are removed entirely; the inner side of the labia minora is scraped and then the vagina is sewn up, leaving only a small hole. The scarred sides actually fuse together. The girls' legs are tied together for two to six weeks to allow healing.

The whole ghastly business is performed without anaesthetic and in unhygienic conditions. The medical complications can be drastic. The young child – or sometimes even a baby – may bleed to death or die of shock from the extreme pain. Later, she may suffer from urinary or reproductive tract infections caused by the obstructed flow of urine and menstrual blood, and various forms of scarring and infertility.

A young teenage girl can only fear marriage. The first time she has intercourse is usually extremely painful. Later, when she has a child, she will have to be opened up with the traditional birthing knife. After the baby is born, she will be sewn up again.

Many women have told me that, as soon as they reach puberty, they fear sexual contact. They often run away when they hear their parents talking about marriage. I've delivered a lot of women who have not been penetrated. The husband has tried his hardest without success, with who-knows-what suffering for his wife, and somehow sperm has found its way up the birth canal to fertilise the egg. And then I've seen situations where they can't be penetrated so their husband opens them with a knife. Women tell me their lives are dominated by two things: fear and pain. Is he coming home tonight? I can hear his footsteps, that's his voice. Yet, for the sake of their name, the name of the clan, their pride as a female, they feel they have to endure circumcision.

*

One of the great myths about FGM is that it's ordained by Islam. The truth is that it's not explicitly endorsed in the Koran at all. One of the few references actually says, 'We have indeed created man[kind] in the best of moulds.'

Advocates of circumcision seize upon a line in the Koran where Mohammad says, 'Do not cut her severely as that is better for a woman and more desirable for a husband.' However, the majority of scholars interpret this as meaning that the Koran does not require anyone to be circumcised. It most likely refers to a minor form of 'trimming' of the clitoral hood, which is done to enhance a woman's sexual pleasure.

APDA has waged a long campaign against FGM, with considerable success. It's essential to get the clan elders and the religious leaders on side. When they hear that FGM is not, in fact, upheld by their religion but comes from an ancient culture that did not respect Allah, they are horrified. Then the women themselves and the traditional birth attendants quickly turn against the practice.

One of our most powerful weapons is a video we made which shows an actual operation. We screen it to isolated communities using a generator to power the projector. Even I, with my medical training, find it horrific to watch. Actors play out a story in which a mother refuses to allow her daughter to be circumcised. Her husband opposes her. As they argue, there's a flashback in which the mother remembers her own experience as a child.

This part of the video shows a real circumcision. The child is about five. Screaming with terror, she is laid on the ground on her back. Two or three women hold her down while others drag her legs apart. The practitioner uses an old-fashioned double-sided razor blade. It seems to take forever as she saws at the little girl. Blood flows copiously from the wound all over the victim, the helpers and onto the ground. The whole time it's going on, the child repeats piteously, 'Help me, Mummy, help me, Mummy, help me, Mummy.' The trouble is, her mummy is one of those holding her legs apart.

The cutting is unbearably painful to watch, but the most horrifying part is when the little girl is sewn up with a thick needle and thread like something you'd use on a chaff bag. The story ends with the mother and her husband taking their argument to the clan leader and the Imam. After pondering the question for a while, these respected leaders tell them that there's no reason why their daughter should be circumcised, and she is saved.

Each time I see this video, I am overcome with anger and revulsion. As it never fails to affect me, I can well imagine the impact it has on new audiences. It's especially important that men see it, as they are the ones with the power to change things.

As a result of our campaigning, FGM is no longer practised in some parts of the Afar region. I believe that in the next decade or so we'll eradicate it entirely.

Most Afar marriages are arranged by the parents. The common tradition is *absuma*, or marriage to the cousin on the groom's mother's side. The woman has absolutely no choice in the matter, while a man is often obligated to marry a certain woman just because she is *absuma*. *Absuma* used to be almost universal but in parts of northern Afar it's changing to favour marriage arranged by consent. The mother and father of the bride are expected to receive a dowry, usually of money and/or livestock. The girl should get clothes, gold and perfume.

If a woman wants to marry another man and she's already married, the man of her choice has to give twelve cows to the husband who divorces her. The divorce takes place first and the new marriage doesn't happen until the divorced husband receives the twelve cows.

If she's widowed, she must marry her former husband's nearest relative, usually his brother. Women have complained to me about this practice, as the man does not take the same responsibility as her previous husband, and can readily divorce his wife, leaving her without any property or children.

I've come across women in some areas who have refused the husband chosen for them by *absuma* and run away. They were caught by their parents, tied up and forced to go ahead with the marriage. In some areas, they've stopped forcing girls to marry very old men. In others, the rules about marrying a deceased husband's brother have been relaxed so that if the widow doesn't want the brother-in-law, she can marry another relative. Either way, the second marriage is obligatory.

It's extremely difficult for a woman to divorce her husband. If there's constant fighting the families may eventually resolve it but, since she is *absuma*, the husband's clan will set conditions whereby she can remarry. This will involve the wife's clan paying a certain number of goats in compensation.

The Koran says that a man may marry up to four wives. Sometimes he takes an additional wife in an area far away from the first. The first wife might not see her husband for a couple of years. She's left to cope with everything by herself. She may have a child or two. Her husband doesn't have any involvement in her life, he's just the man she's married to, and he's far away with the other wife, or he may have even married a third. She may go through any number of difficulties by herself. The child, or children, might get sick, some of the herd might die and he's not there. He keeps her dangling on a chain. He figures she'll be looked after by her relatives. Afar women find polygamy very hard to bear.

*

Generally, women lead a very hard life. They perform 85 per cent of all household tasks. It's they who bear and raise the children. They fetch the water, often walking for hours each day with a baby on their back, perhaps leading a couple more children who may barely be past toddler stage. They fill a goatskin from the well or waterhole and sling it up onto their back underneath the baby, tying it with cords over the shoulders.

The women spend hours each day grinding grain for *ga'ambo*. This is mixed with water and cooked in a hole in the ground, the sides of which are lined with flat stones. They light a fire in the hole, then cover it with layers of damp cloth to keep the heat in. They mould the bread into flat cakes and, after about half an hour, when the fire has died down to red-hot coals, they slap the cakes onto the rock sides, where they stick.

Another of the women's jobs is milking goats. The milk can be poured into a goatskin bag, which is hung on a frame. Then it's rocked back and forth for an hour or more to make butter. The women, or often children as young as four or five, look after the goats. Men look after camels and cattle, and handle such things as the sale of livestock and buying supplies for the household.

With their poor diet and their crippling workload, poor pastoral women are in a perpetual state of near-exhaustion. One of APDA's aims is to break down this terrible inequality. As with most injustices, education is the answer. But it's a tricky business. Before the woman can be educated, the men have to agree to it. When we approach a community, the clan elders will have a meeting to discuss the proposal. It's often very hard to persuade them that educating women is a good idea. In the early days, when I started doing this work, they regarded me with deep suspicion. They didn't think much of a white person – a white *woman* – telling them how they should run their lives. Nowadays, even people in the most remote parts of the Afar have heard of Maalika, and they know that I'm doing it for them.

Today, the front-line troops in women's education are our women extension workers. They're the ones who have to do the initial persuading. One of our most powerful tools is a film which was made by an Addis-based production company using Afar actors. It shows the day-to-day life of a typical nomadic family. We see them setting up camp, the woman fetching water, grinding grain, making bread, keeping the goats together, looking after the children, churning butter. Her husband, meanwhile, wanders off to the village to visit his mates and to chew *chat*, a plant which acts as an amphetamine.

The woman is pregnant. While she's at the waterhole, she begins to have a miscarriage. Friends help her back to her *deboita*. By the time her husband arrives home, she has bled to death.

When I write this down, it sounds a bit corny. But the standard of acting, camera work and direction are first class. The amateur actors invest their parts with a truth that comes from their own experience. Even sophisticated westerners who see it are moved; it's impossible not to be. When Afar men see it, they often recognise for the first time an injustice which has been going on in front of them all their lives.

I helped make the film. Ten days after it was shot, I was visiting Eli Daar, and virtually the same scenario happened in real life. One of my health workers came to town looking for me. He said, 'Quickly, Maalika, I have a woman in the bush and she's dying. She's bleeding. I don't know what more to do with her.'

We hurriedly set off in our four-wheel drive. After travelling for a few hours through the desert, we found an eight months' pregnant woman who'd lost a vast amount of blood. She'd gone to collect water. While she was coming back with the container strapped to her back, she'd started bleeding. The health worker had told her to lie down and rest. She lay down, then thought to herself, I've only collected one container of water. We should have another one for today. She collected the second one and came back with blood pouring from her.

She was utterly anaemic to the point where she was breathless. The inside of her eyes and lips were white. Her pulse was racing and she was breathing so fast she couldn't talk. I asked her family where they wanted me to take her. There were two hospitals we could have gone to, at Dubte and Dessie, both of them many hours' drive away. I had no confidence Dubte would give her appropriate treatment. I suggested Dessie. Her family asked instead to go to Djibouti because they had relatives there who'd pay for the hospital treatment. The driving distance to the nearest hospital in Djibouoti was about the same as to Dessie.

I loaned them our vehicle and told them to load it with some of her close relatives. I instructed them, 'When you get to the hospital, you'll have to give blood. Don't change your mind when you get there; promise you'll give blood to help her.'

They agreed. As they got in the car, the woman's first son was crying. She'd had another son who'd died. I said, 'Don't worry, I'll bring Mummy back to you.' But Mummy never came back. When they got to Galaafi on the border the officials on the Djibouti side made a fuss about the car. They took ages to fill in all the documents that were required. While they were doing it, she died.

Reading over what I have written, I see that I may have painted an unsympathetic picture of the Afar. Some of their customs are harsh, no doubt – how could they be otherwise, living in the environment they do? It's all too easy to depict them as primitives whose culture is inferior to those in the developed world.

Their reputation has not been helped by the writings of a

British explorer, Wilfred Thesiger. Thesiger was born in 1910 at the British Legation in Addis Ababa. He spent his early years in what was then Abyssinia. He was educated at Eton and Oxford, and in 1930 he went back to Addis to attend the coronation of Haile Selassie.

Afterwards, he spent a month hunting in the Danakil desert, which led him, three years later, to mount an expedition to explore the Awash River to its end. He published the story of this adventure in a book, *The Danakil Diary*.

I've read it. A lot of it is about Thesiger killing things. He writes endlessly, with typical British ruling-class arrogance, about shooting wild animals and birds. He seems to have spent every day taking potshots at anything that moved. He occasionally laments the fact that he'd only wounded some poor creature and it had disappeared into the bush. What bothered him was not the animal's suffering, but the fact that he'd missed out on a trophy.

The central theme of Thesiger's book is that the Afar are a savage and bloodthirsty people who kill strangers on sight. He alleges that an Afar man's tribal status depended on the number of enemy warriors he had killed and castrated. A man was not a man unless he had done this at least once, according to Thesiger.

Ismael, and every Afar I've spoken to about it, say that this is absolute twaddle. They contend that Thesiger was misled by his Oromo guides. In fact, it was the Oromo who used to castrate their enemies. When I talk to the old men about Thesiger's claims, they laugh. 'Castration? We can take you to an Afar castrated by Oromo.' Even today, the Afar are having a hard time living down Mr Thesiger's stories.

I love and respect the Afar. They're the most peaceful people I've ever met. I've been through Sudan, Somalia, Saudi Arabia all by myself, and in many places I've felt vulnerable as a woman. I've had a few unpleasant and potentially dangerous experiences, but never once with the Afar. I stay for weeks at a time in the distant desert, without my husband, and I've never so much as received a snide comment. The Afar have always shown me incredible respect.

Whereas we in the west are concerned with individual wealth and status, their focus is on the community. I once said to Ismael, 'What would you do if you had money?'

'What sort of a question is that?' he replied. 'You know there are Afar here. It's already spent.'

If an Afar confides in you that he or she has a problem, then you are obliged either to do something to help or else find someone who can. This is why there are always people staying with us wherever we live.

There are traditional laws which bind the Afar to assist one another. For instance, if goats are lost in drought or through disease, there are ways of helping those who are poor, combining traditional custom and Islamic teaching. There are rigid rules about the number of goats and camels and so on that constitutes wealth. The Afar classify poverty according to the number of animals that you have left. Every year, anyone above that poverty line gives a certain percentage of their household goods at the end of Ramadan. The Sheik will distribute it to the poor. There is no such thing as a wealthy Afar; at least, no one with the kind of wealth that you see elsewhere in Ethiopia.

Highland Ethiopians think the Afar way is a laughable system. They are classic capitalists – everyone is out for themselves and market forces rule. Of course, practically the whole world has embraced the capitalist system. A few get rich at the expense of many. I believe that if we ran things according to Afar thinking, we would completely eradicate poverty.

*

Afar thinking is not linear. They don't have the same concept of time as other Ethiopians. It's part of their nomadism. Because of this, they have a problem fitting in with the western work ethic. They get criticised because, in Afar society, no one is employed, they only have their animals to worry about. All this town stuff is new to them. People say the Afar never work, but I've seen them literally breaking up a hillside to make a road, led by the Sheik chanting for them, while the women at the bottom of the hill were keeping them supplied with water and *shahi*. They work together fantastically if they have to get something done, but they're not good at turning up at the office at nine sharp. The Afar way of life is reasonable and healthy, though. Tension and high blood pressure and competition are unknown.

Lateral thinking is one of the things I love about them. Still, APDA doesn't run the Afar way because I work under extreme pressure from our donors. I'm juggling the two cultures and I have to try to please both.

The Afar have their own legal systems for solving disputes. Crime is customarily regarded as relating to three organs of the body. Offences are either committed by the tongue, the hands or the genitals. The criteria for measuring crimes depends on whether the offender acknowledges his misdeed and responds positively. The punishment depends on whether the action was accidental or premeditated. For each kind of crime, there are set fines and punishments laid down by tradition. If the crime is regarded as deliberate, then the accused must be punished. This can consist of being beaten or having his animals slaughtered, depending on the severity of the offence.

Crimes and disputes are subject to the *mablo*, or traditional judgement. This system has evolved over hundreds and hundreds of years. It's far older than the British adversarial system.

Say you and I fight. I insult you, and you take this as a bad thing. My clan will pull me away from you, and your clan will pull you away from me. My clan will tell me not to show my face: 'Keep quiet, we're handling this.' Your clan will do the same. Then two lots of clan elders will sit down for a judgement.

They do what they call the 'weighing of words'. Who spoke the first word? Was the word said in anger? Was the word said in revenge? Was the word said in jealousy? How was this word formed and where did it come from?

Nothing in the *mablo* is written down. An oral recorder chants the last sound of every sentence, and by that means it's locked in his mind. At the end of the discussion, if someone wants to recall part of the evidence the recorder will get up and repeat it perfectly – he has no tape recorder, no pen and paper, nothing – they can remember two or three hours of testimony this way.

The elders are very experienced. If anybody's lying, they will find out, and, in the end, that person will have to confess. Eventually they'll make a decision – 'She did it, she provoked this. She did it out of anger, this is out of line.'

Then they vote on the judgement. Is the judgement a true judgement or not? If anybody says they don't see truth in this judgement, then the elders have to do it all again.

At the end of the judgement two things seal it. I must kiss you in a way that humiliates me – on the forehead – then ask forgiveness from everyone in the room. The elders pray that this will never happen again, that the lips will be controlled, that the tongue will be stilled, that the anger will not fall on the ground like this anymore and make a mess.

Then the news is distributed throughout the clans. The judgement has landed, the person has been punished. Then they do the *mikla*, or payment of punishment. The penalty is set by traditional law – how many goats, how many cows, how many camels I've got to pay you. And I *have* to pay. If I can't, my clan must pay, otherwise my clan's name will be disgraced.

I attended one *mablo* in Afdera for a murder which had been committed 30 years previously. Two young men of about sixteen or eighteen years old were angry at one another. First, they pushed and shoved, and eventually one killed the other. I don't know why it took so long, but for 30 years the men's clans had been looking for a judgement.

The alleged murderer was middle aged by now. He was found guilty and handed over to the other clan with the judgement, 'Kill him now or accept payment for the damage.' The traditional fine for a murder is 100 camels or the equivalent in money. They decided to take the payment.

The handover took place by a river. Hundreds of people from each clan gathered. The guilty clan killed camels to feed them and women were cooking bread. When they handed over the payment there was great relief on both sides. Even the losing side was happy. One said to me, 'We were praying to God for so long, now we can have peace.'

We use the *mablo* system for resolution of disputes within APDA. One of our men is a leader in this sort of judgement. He can do the reciting, he can weigh the words up, and come back like a good judge and make a decision.

Although women don't normally take part in the *mablo*, an Afar elder once asked me to appear in one. Médecins sans Frontières had set up a TB project with the Gala'ah clan. The people were behaving very badly. They'd got into a tussle with MSF because they wanted control of the project, thinking that they'd get money.

I'd tried to stop the fight myself. It had boiled down to an argument between one faction who wanted to keep arguing and another who wanted them to behave. MSF were excluded from the *mablo* because they weren't Afar, but the elders wanted me to give evidence because I'd been involved.

I told the old man who had asked me, 'No, it's men's business. I can't take part.'

He said, 'But what you have to say is vital because you can prove this case. You know. You've seen it.'

I demurred again and he said, 'But what's the problem?'

'I told you, because I'm not a man.'

'What?' He looked surprised. 'But you're not a woman.'

I said, 'Listen, get off my back – what am I, then? I've got a child, I gave birth to her. What am I? Tell me.'

'We're confused, we don't know. You're not a woman and you're not a man.'

'So I'm between, am I?'

He laughed. 'We don't know, but please, get into the *mablo* and say your piece. We need to get this thing cleared up.'

So I did, and it was.

CHAPTER 15

In 1997 APDA established a proper base in Assaita on the banks of the beautiful Awash River. The organisation was growing so large that it was no longer possible to operate out of friends' houses. The compound looked out over the river to rich agricultural land where the Kurubuda people live. It was a peaceful rural scene with date palms and fruit trees, a range of pale hills painted across the horizon in the distance. Down on the banks of the river, monkeys played. In the evening we'd watch enchanting sunsets and see the water birds flying in formation across the sky to their nesting places.

When we first went there the only building we had was a house. We added a couple of sheds for vehicles and stores, then an office building and a shelter for meetings. On higher ground we put down a cement slab and that was where the men prayed. In summer we also slept there in the open air.

I built myself a *deboita* a bit away from the rest of the buildings. It was going to be my little retreat, but I didn't have it for long. The men just took it over, and put dirty shoes and socks and junk in there.

*

We kept our house in Addis Ababa, as we still needed a base in the capital. Aisha started going to an international kindergarten where the pupils were a mixture of Ethiopians and expatriates. Ismael and I tried to be in Addis as much as possible, but our work was in the Afar, and a lot of the time Aisha was left with the housegirl to look after her.

When we needed to travel between our two homes we'd go to a truck station and find someone heading in the direction we wanted to go. It could take up to fourteen hours to make the journey in a heavily laden vehicle, either sitting crammed into the cab with three or four passengers, or in the back in the open air.

Along the way we sometimes used to spend the night at a run-down hotel in Gewwaane. It was called Total because it was behind a Total service station. One night there was a tremendous commotion from a room a few doors away from us. A guest had taken his evening meal into his room and put it down on the floor where he intended to eat it. Before he began he decided to go to the toilet. He left his room, leaving the door ajar. While he was out a hyena had slipped inside, attracted by the smell of food. He came back in, shut and locked the door, then turned around and spotted the beast. Don't ask me why he didn't see it when he first walked in. Anyway, both hyena and guest reacted with panic. The hyena badly wanted to get out of there. The guest had no argument with that, but in his haste he couldn't get his key into the lock. Whilst he scrabbled frantically at the door yelling for help at the top of his voice, the hyena tore around the room, peeing and defecating with fear.

Alerted by the commotion, hotel staff came running and arrived just as the terrified man at last found the lock. The door was flung open and he burst into the corridor. They were just recovering from that when the hyena followed, skidded between their legs, and disappeared outside into the night.

*

Some Afar areas are almost in a state of war because of Issa tribesmen migrating from the areas they occupy in Ethiopia and Djibouti, and grazing their herds on Afar land. Armed clashes are frequent, and in the dangerous areas men never go anywhere without carrying a rifle. Former Ethiopian army Kalashnikovs are the weapon of choice.

On one occasion I was travelling with Aisha from Addis to Assaita in the back of a truck which was picking up and putting down passengers along the way. At one stop half a dozen Issa got on board. They were wearing red headbands, which signified that they were fighters, and carrying guns.

They were young men, cocky and swaggering, boasting loudly to one another about how they'd taken land from the Afar. I was very uncomfortable about sharing the same transport with them. I knew Afar who'd been attacked by Issa and I'd heard many stories about their ruthless behaviour. I kept my head down and avoided eye contact. Then Aisha, who was about four, suddenly piped up in Afar, 'Mama, I need some water.'

I tried to get her to be quiet, without making it too obvious, but she didn't see the danger. 'Mummy,' she insisted, 'I'm thirsty. Can't I have a drink?'

The Issa stopped talking and gave us a hard stare. 'Are you Afar?' said one.

I assured him that we were not. He was about to say something more when we pulled into a truck stop. We watched in astonishment as all the Issa got down, sauntered over to a stationary truck on the other side of the road and held it up!

This hostility with the Issa is ruining a lot of Afar communities. Recently, the head of our women extension workers in Gewwaane, a very dedicated woman named Haalima, reported an increasing incidence of maternal deaths in one of her settlements. Eight women had died in a month, and about 30 children and babies were suffering from malnutrition.

I sent one of our vehicles to her with some cases of baby food, and when I found the time a week or so later, I went to see the situation for myself. About 20 kilometres from our destination we passed a squalid little village of around 50 dwellings. Scrap paper and plastic bags blew about in the wind. Groups of men and youths sat idly around. The houses were not the dome-shaped *deboitas* of an Afar village, but square huts made of sticks and mud. Haalima had told me that this Issa village was a breeding ground for killers who were raiding the nearby Afar.

A little further on we stopped at Haalima's house. She and her family lived in one room in a small concrete building which we use to store medical and educational supplies. She was sitting in the shade of the verandah with her baby, her mother and brother. She rose to her feet, a tall, very beautiful woman, dressed in an exuberantly coloured dress and head cloth, wearing a traditional necklace of red and blue beads. Her perfectly white teeth were filed into points. She was as immaculate as if she'd just stepped out the front door of a luxury apartment in the city. We kissed each other's hands and sat in the shade to talk.

Haalima is one of our best people. She's a teacher as well as an extension worker. She has to travel up to 100 kilometres away from where she lives to cover her territory. An NGO which operates in the area, Farm Africa, has pledged to help her with transport, but they never have, so she gets about by cadging lifts.

The settlement she was concerned with was about five minutes away. We waited a few minutes while our driver, Hussein, said his prayers, then we got into the Land Cruiser and rattled off over a rough dirt road. Most Afar settlements consist of just a few *deboitas*. This one was like a permanent village of 30 or more. There were hardly any men about. Haalima explained that they'd taken their animals some distance away because the Issa had stolen their grazing land. The women and children who were left lived in constant fear of being raided.

Rather than scatter and move away from the Issa threat, the clan had decided to consolidate into one large community. But this brought its own problems. One of them was sanitation: the people were living in the midst of their own waste. The other and most immediate problem was that they were starving. Because the animals were far away it was difficult to get access to milk.

Haalima told me that the baby food had made a difference but there were still many malnourished children. I took a tape measure and did a house-to-house survey, measuring children's biceps to see if they were developing according to their age. I discovered that one in five children had malnutrition. I saw many with eye and skin diseases, and a lot of anaemia. One three-year-old couldn't stand up, she was so malnourished.

Haalima said that there were many more settlements in her area which were suffering from the same problems.

I was mystified – well, not really mystified as I'd seen this sort of thing so often. Angry is a better word, because there was a government health clinic only a couple of kilometres away and an international NGO was operating in the area.

We went to the clinic. The director was a clean, well-dressed, well-padded fellow who was not Afar. He was a highlander and didn't even speak the local language. Because he'd been educated, we conversed in English. He told me a familiar tale. He said that a while ago they took about 30 children from the settlement to an MSF clinic in Galaaha, 200 kilometres away. The MSF people gave them food and treatment. They were all fine now, he said.

I told him I'd just been to the village and they were far from fine. He shrugged. I knew what was going on here. As long as they knew we were looking after the settlement, the government people wouldn't need to worry about it.

'What about the other settlements?' I asked him. 'You could send some field workers.'

I suspected I'd know the answer to this one, too. The workers were demanding a per diem payment on top of their usual salary before they'd go into the field. He didn't have the money to pay them.

By now I was beginning to get heated. These were people's lives we were dealing with here. On the wall, there were nicely drawn graphs showing things like, 'SEASONAL VARIATION OF THE FOUR TOP DISEASES OF MORBIDITY', and 'MAKE YOUR WORKING ENVIRONMENT CLEAN AND SIGHTY' [sic]. It certainly was all very nice and clean *but they were not doing anything*!

He listened to me without a trace of discomfort while I exploded. He told me smoothly not to worry. Thanks to APDA's baby food, it was all under control now.

But I knew it wasn't under control. And I knew that the Afar wouldn't bring their sick children to this clinic, because they were afraid they'd have to speak Amharic or that they'd want them to buy medicine that they couldn't afford, or that they'd be patronised and treated with contempt. They never tell them what's wrong in these clinics. Instead, they spout nonsense such as, 'The wind got into you,' meaning that the wind has caused the disease. This is a terrible policy. If you're honest with people about what's wrong with them, then they'll learn to do something about it.

I calmed down eventually. We shook hands politely with the director and left. I discovered later that the NGO which was supposed to be helping these people had 'other priorities' than malnutrition. They were interested in malaria and trachoma. I told them that people were dying and they couldn't afford to pick and choose.

I called a meeting with the boss of the Area Health Bureau. He still insisted that there was no problem.

In the end, I resigned myself to sending more baby food for the foreseeable future. The trouble is that the Afar don't know their rights. They should be standing up and shouting and making a fuss. Someone has to do it and, until they've been educated, that someone will have to be me.

When he was 60 years old, my father had become an Anglican priest. He served for five years in a parish at Nundle, in country New South Wales. Then he and my mother moved to Moss Vale to be close to my brother David. David lived in nearby Bowral, where he practised as an obstetrician/gynaecologist.

One night I had a vivid dream about my father, in which I saw him looking extremely pale and afraid of death. It was as if he were standing right in front of me. The dream was so powerful that it was still with me when I woke up. I told Ismael I was worried that Father was in trouble. I thought about it a lot for the next few days. I didn't have the money to call home to see if everything was all right. Then a letter came from my sister Rosemary. She said that Father had had a serious nosebleed which he couldn't stop. Mother had put him in her car, with David following behind, and they'd taken him to the local hospital. Because the bleed was high in his nostril, they couldn't deal with it in the country hospital. They'd gone to two more before they found one which could treat him. He'd needed a transfusion. When I checked the date of the letter, it had happened at exactly the time I'd had my dream.

In his early eighties Father had contracted bladder cancer. The doctors said it was quite manageable and it wasn't going to kill him. He became obsessed by his diet, and in his last years he was very difficult to look after. Mother always wanted the best for him. She'd cook him things that he especially liked, then he'd refuse to eat. He had always been exacting and calculating. He kept to the Biblical idea that he would live for four score years and ten, and I believe that he literally willed himself to die once he approached this milestone. Mother found this extraordinarily hard to cope with.

David helped as much as he could. Mother remained the obedient, loyal wife until one day when David arrived and she said, 'This is way beyond you, it's way beyond me, it's way beyond anybody.'

They put Father in a local hospital where his condition deteriorated further. I received a telegram from home telling me that he was dying. I walked from our home in Shola Makananya to the Médecins sans Frontières office to call David. When I got through, he told me that Father had died. It was 19 January 1998. He was 87.

I was devastated. Father had been distant and difficult; I often thought he didn't understand me or what I was doing. Yet, he had still been my father. I could see all too clearly parts of his personality in me – especially his stubbornness.

I put the telephone down and relayed the news to Ismael. He comforted me. Then he did a wonderful thing – he went and fetched my Bible. 'Here,' he said. 'You need this.'

As usual, we were living hand-to-mouth. I didn't go home for the funeral. We couldn't afford it.

CHAPTER 16

I'm always being asked how a Christian and a Muslim can be married. Ismael gets the same question all the time. I don't think any human can convert another human. It's utter nonsense to think that when you're married to someone you can change your religion because of them. It means you didn't have a belief in the first place.

The fundamental extreme is ugly in any religion because things get out of balance: you exaggerate one thing only and forget about the rest. I don't think a relationship with God is about changing people. I'm not going to change Ismael, just as I'm probably not going to convert the Afar people single-handedly. I pray for them all the time, but then, if I lived in Australia I'd be praying for the people there.

I think sometimes of Christ's words, 'No one comes to the Father except through me.' If I'm to interpret this literally, it means that no one who has not been saved will be allowed into the kingdom of heaven. In the end, whether my husband is Muslim or whether he's a secular materialist from the western world, biblically there's no difference. If I marry a person who has not committed his life to Christ – that's the problem.

I've cried to God about this. Was I disobedient? I believe that there's a reason to hope not. I don't want to sound pious but I honestly believe there's a purpose for this marriage. I believe it's for the Afar, and because it's for the Afar and not me, I can't question it. No one ever stops me from being Christian. I'd be foolish if I doubted now, after all these years, that God has a purpose for Ismael and for any of the Afar whom I know. I know there are plenty of dogmatists in the Church who would disagree with me, but I really don't think Ismael's religion is relevant.

I think of the poor fellow who was a thief on the cross beside Jesus. At the very last moment before he died he was promised he'd be with Christ in heaven. Nothing's black and white. A lot of people in religion try to stick everything in boxes – you're wrong, I'm right. This is condemnation. Who can condemn, other than God? Not me, for heaven's sake. I'll be the next one to be condemned if I criticise. We can't underestimate God for any reason and we shouldn't try to manipulate other people's lives.

I think a lot of missionary work is manipulative. In my mind, I'm not sure about mission services. I think anybody can have a mission. Say you live in Bondi or Vaucluse, you have an ordinary life, you go to the office, you come home, you have three kids, you're a member of a few clubs ... if you live out a godly life amongst these people, that is your mission. You don't have to buy a plane ticket to a foreign country.

The west, as much as any place in the world, still needs to hear the message of Christ. I reckon the way the Afar live is a few kilometres, if you can talk in kilometres, closer to God than half the western world in terms of morality – and they're Muslim. They have an incredible way of determining how one ought to behave and they stick to it, as opposed to the western way, which is every man for himself.

I'm lucky that Ismael is such a tolerant man. When I've been troubled, such as when I was grieving for my father, Ismael would bring me my Bible and say, 'Come on, you've got to read this, you've got to stop this.' Wherever we've lived he's found me a church to go to. He's a good man, my husband. I can't imagine being married to anyone else; he's perfect for me. In the last few years he's even begun showing affection towards me in public. If I'm about to go away on a trip, he'll put his arms around me and kiss me on the neck, saying, 'In the name of God may she go in safety.' It's a radical thing to do but the other Afar accept it because we've all been through so much together.

When we get up in the morning, I usually sit quietly for a few minutes and read my Bible. In the other corner of the room, Ismael will pray, facing the north. Ismael left it completely up to Aisha to decide whether she wanted to be Christian or Muslim. When she was a toddler, she used to imitate her daddy when he was doing his devotions, and often tumble over flat on her face. When she was little she thought for a while she'd like to be a Muslim, but now she's decided to be a Christian, and Ismael's happy with that. Both Aisha and our son, Rammid, were baptised in St Matthew's Anglican Church in Addis Ababa.

I'm blessed more than any European I know because I have the privilege of living and knowing what most of the world is really like. Most of the world isn't the west. I know exactly what poverty is and that's an extraordinarily large privilege.

There's no European I know who lives like I do, because my husband put me straight into his lifestyle. Most Europeans who marry an African live in what I call 'Quasiland' – between one culture and another. I've met plenty of western women who say they have a West African husband, for instance, and they're coping very well with two cultures. That's rubbish. They're not living in this culture. They live in Addis Ababa; they're employed by some company, or the UN or an embassy; they have more insurance than in their own country; they live behind high fences, with all the facilities of the west in their houses, plus they import their food; they continually visit the west; they don't even have to speak to the local people because they have someone to do the shopping.

Despite my questions, in the end I'm always reminded that my marriage is right. I still don't know why I should be married to Ismael and maybe I won't know until the day I die. But there is a reason. Life is never an easy cruise, never a straight line or a road without bumps. It's up and down. I've had some big downs and I've begged God to get me out of this. 'Put me back where I should be,' I pray. 'You know where I was born; you know the life I came from, God, so why don't you put me back there? Give me what I knew, I've had enough of this, I can't go on.'

Each time the answer is definite: 'No. I'm giving you all that you need, so why are you getting this whole thing wrong?' And I get strength again to go on. He gives me just enough of a glimmer of hope to get through it and push on, and somehow I rise up again. But I don't think God ever allows me to rise up high enough so as to say, 'Look, I've made it.'

Ismael and I have some lively discussions about religion. Recently, we saw on television yet another atrocity in Iraq. A bomb had gone off and dozens of people had been killed. I can't even remember the details, these things have become so commonplace. Ismael said to me, 'If we're going to believe in the Christian God, I don't understand where this God is at this minute. Where is this God? How the hell does this George Bush get away with invading this country? We don't have anything left in the Middle East that he hasn't touched.'

George Bush thinks he has God on his side. At the same time, many of these atrocities are being committed in the name of Allah. So there's a lot of confusion about God on both sides.

I've decided that being in Ethiopia with Ismael is where I

belong. It's been a gradual thing. I've had some terrible times of depression. I still have moments of extreme tiredness when I don't know where to turn. I know a tiredness where every muscle in my body is in pain, when I don't know what I'm going to do with myself and that unless I meet a deadline I'm cutting some community short. In the strength of God, I can pick up again. The good thing is that God doesn't give me all highs. There are troughs and highs. I never get to the top of the mountain. If I did, I'm such a human being that I'd go off the rails. That's the thing that keeps me on track, I think: God never lets me leave reality.

Where we live now, there's only an Ethiopian Orthodox church. The services are in a special language, *Geez*, which is used only for religious occasions. I don't understand it so there's not much point in my going.

I miss church. But I can remember hymns from back in my childhood. When I'm without my Bible, I can recall bits of Scripture. I've learnt that prayer is more than just a ritual. You can be praying silently as you go about daily life, and if I didn't have that communication with God I'd go mad.

In the end, it all comes down to tolerance. One time when someone asked Ismael how he could marry a Christian, he laughed and said, 'Well, I'm doing the right thing, aren't I? If she's right, when she goes to heaven she'll pull me in after her, and if I'm right I'll pull her in.'

I agree with something my brother George once said: 'When we get into heaven, we'll be surprised who we see.'

CHAPTER 17

Early in 1999, I was walking along a foot track in Assaita town just after sunset with one of APDA's health workers, Abdu Hamadu. I felt a sharp jab on my foot. I had disturbed a snake hidden in the shrubbery beside the track.

Abdu knew that I shouldn't try to walk, as any movement would speed up my blood circulation. He picked me up and carried me to a friend's house close to where I'd been bitten. He then found an Oxfam car which, purely by coincidence, was in town.

The nearest hospital was Dubte, about 60 kilometres away. By the time the car had arrived I was drifting in and out of consciousness. My leg and back were swollen with blood, and I was bleeding from my nose and mouth. The venom stops blood from clotting. I was about to bleed to death internally.

My friends gently put me in the back and set off for Dubte. The journey was like a surreal nightmare. I knew I was in a car and we were going to the hospital. I was worried about what to do with Aisha. In my semi-lucid moments, I thought I should leave a message for her. I should give my message to one of my sisters because Aisha is a girl and it wouldn't be easy for Ismael to bring her up. Which sister should I give the message to? That was hard. I couldn't quite decide. I remember asking for a pen but, when I tried to write, I fell unconscious again.

By the time I arrived at the hospital, word had got back to APDA. One of Ismael's clan elders was waiting, demanding that they hand me over to him so that he could give me traditional Afar snakebite medicine. As I lay there in an oddly detached state, I could hear him insisting, 'In the name of holy God, give me the woman, I am in charge, I am her representative.' There were people in white coats . . . a syringe drifted in and out of my vision . . . I was vaguely aware of an argument . . . someone saying, 'No, we're going to inject her.' Then there was a sting and they pushed the antivenin into a muscle.

I spent about ten days lying in a house owned by a woman from Ismael's clan. Oddly enough, even when I thought I might be dying I had no particular regrets. I've come to have the same attitude to death as the Afar, that it's utterly inevitable and part of everything. My main concern was still which of my sisters would be the best person to look after Aisha and how I could tell Ismael.

In the end, the hospital staff managed to convince the clan elder that they could handle the situation. The circulation in my foot is still not good. I don't know if the traditional medicine would have helped, but the Afar swear that it does. There are also special leaves which are said to protect you. They smell like camphor, and they say that snakes hate them so much that if you carry them in your pocket, you'll never be bitten.

In my regular letters home I was always careful to tone down the accounts of my more hair-raising experiences. While my father was alive there had now and then been suggestions that he and Mother would come to Ethiopia for a visit. I'd always side-stepped the issue because I was certain that Father wouldn't approve of the way I was living. A year after he died, Mother asked again if she could come. She was 82 years old. Just making the long plane journey to Ethiopia would deter most people her age, but Mother was one of the fittest 82-year-olds around and, in her quiet way, very determined.

After a family meeting, George offered to come with her and, in June 1999, Ismael, Aisha and I went out to the airport at Addis Ababa to meet them. We'd given a lot of thought to how we could give them a taste of Ethiopian life without tiring Mother too much. We planned to show her around Addis, take her on picnics to the Entoto Mountains, find some local entertainment for her to see – nothing too strenuous.

As usual, the house was full of people – about fifteen or so, as I recall. Mother was quite taken aback when she saw my kitchen with two Primus stoves on the floor. 'Oh dear, Valerie, I didn't bring you up like this. You don't even have a table to prepare food. Never mind, I'll find you one.'

After Mother and George had had a wash and a bit of a rest, the housegirl made us all some *shahi*. We sat in the main room, where there *was* a table, to discuss our plans.

'Where's the car?' asked Mother.

'What car?' said Ismael.

'Why, the car that's taking us to the Afar region.'

Ismael said to me in Afar, 'You never told me about this.'

'I didn't know,' I replied. 'It's the middle of the hot season, she can't go to the Afar.'

Mother said, 'What are you two busy talking about?'

'Mother, we've got a plan for you, it's going to be fine, and we're going to spend all the time with you that you need. But the Afar region is burning hot now, it's 40, 45 and over. It's too hot for you and too hot for George. It'd be silly to go there. Let's have a good time around Addis.'

'I don't like the way you're talking, dear. I came to see you and the work; now, please get the car here.'

Ismael rang a friend who had a car. He said, 'I know you're busy, Ilyas, but come round and pretend you're going to give me the car – just show it.'

Ilyas brought his car around. Like most cars in Ethiopia, it had dents on every panel, the tyres were bald, and the upholstery looked as if it had been used to transport livestock – which quite possibly it had.

Mother looked it over critically, but still was not in the least discouraged. 'Hmmm, it's not much of a car but I suppose we'll get there.'

We reached Awash on the first day without incident and spent the night in a hotel. On the following day, as we headed for Assaita, we passed a herd of cattle being driven alongside the road. Ismael took a look at them and asked Ilyas to stop. They sat speaking to one another in Afar, stealing glances now and then at the cattle.

'What's the matter?' said Mother. 'Why have we stopped?'

I said, 'They're just talking about that mob of cattle over there. They look like they're being driven by Issa. Ismael thinks they've stolen them.'

Ismael and Ilyas opened their doors and began walking across towards the herd. Mother said, 'Now what's going to happen?'

'Oh, Ismael will probably be in jail tonight.'

We watched as they approached the herdsmen and spoke to them. They talked for quite a while then came back, roaring with laughter.

Mother said, 'Now what's happening?'

'It's all right. It's Afar herdsmen who've pinched Issa cattle.'

*

We didn't yet have a proper place to live in the compound, so we'd been making do in the office. Mother wasn't at all fazed by the basic conditions – not even by the toilet, which dropped straight into the Awash River. On our first night it was so hot everyone slept outside. We gave Mother a folding camp bed.

In the middle of the night a gale force wind tore through the compound enveloping everything in choking dust. You could barely breathe or see more than a metre or so in front of your face. I shouted to everybody to get into the office and asked one of the boys to fold up Mother's bed.

'No, I can't go in,' said Mother.

'Come on, Mother. The wind's only going to get worse.'

She kept saying she couldn't go in and then finally came out with what was bothering her. 'Dear, I can't go anywhere until I've found my teeth.' She'd put them under her pillow and now they'd blown away somewhere.

We got all the boys who were living in the compound to take torches and look for the missing teeth. Poor Mother, she was terrified that someone was going to tread on them. Eventually, they were found and rinsed off, and we all had a good laugh. But it was quite traumatic for her at the time.

Over the next few days we took her to see the health and education programs and to meet some of our key people. She was interested in everything, questioning people through a translator, wanting to know the most minute details.

When we returned to Addis she took another look at my kitchen and asked Ismael to take her to a carpenter. She had two little tables made up, one to put the cookers on, the other to prepare food, and presented them to me as a gift. What luxury.

It was wonderful to be able to spend time with her. We had one or two long talks, just the two of us. She told me all about my father's last days, and she left me in no doubt about her support for my work and my marriage. 'I don't know why God gave you such a good husband,' she said, 'and I hope you realise that. You're all right, but your husband's pretty wonderful.'

She and George spent a fortnight with us. The visit was a great success. It was the best thing Mother could have done as, for the remaining years of her life, whenever I wrote to her she was able to visualise what I was doing.

In that same year, 1999, I was awarded the Order of Australia. Mother went to Canberra to collect the medal. She was probably a lot more excited about it than I was. I'm not even too sure where it is. I think it's in a drawer somewhere in the office in Addis Ababa.

Two years later we began making plans for another visit to Australia. I wrote to my relatives and told them that we'd be there in September. I left it up to Ismael to organise the travel arrangements. September arrived and the days passed by without any arrangements being made. Ten days before we were due to be in Australia, Ismael was roaming around the Afar region completely out of contact. In my usual impetuous fashion, I suddenly decided that I'd waited long enough. I shouted around the compound for Waasi. We call him 'The Cowboy', because he'll do anything no matter how difficult or dangerous it might be.

Waasi said, 'What's the matter, Maalika, are you in trouble?'

'I want to get this crazy husband of mine back here. He's somewhere out near Afdera.' The last I'd heard, Ismael had taken off down the Afdera road to look at a water dam we were building.

There were no vehicles in the Assaita compound but that didn't deter Waasi. He went into town and gate-crashed a meeting of the Regional Council. He borrowed one of their pickups and off we went, heading for Afdera, 500 kilometres away.

It was a shocking road. As we bounced along, I was fuming. We couldn't leave my relatives wondering if we were coming or not any longer. We had to get things organised. Near Afdera, I saw Ismael's vehicle, a clapped-out old Nissan that we'd bought on the cheap, pulled up beside the road. All of our vehicles had names. This one was called *Wasso Mali*, which means, 'going without any borders'.

We pulled up and Ismael's driver came over. 'I can't thank God enough,' he said. 'I was about to die out here under this scorching sun. Every tyre is blown. There's no water or anything to eat here.'

Ismael was sitting serenely under a tree with a couple of old men, sipping coffee. He gave me a languid wave. I walked over to him and said, 'What's going on here?'

'Me and these men are having coffee.'

'Ismael, do you know what date it is today?'

'No, what is it?'

'It's ten days before you and me and Aisha are meant to be in Australia.'

'Yes, I thought about that. I thought we'd go a bit later.'

'That's no good. My relatives are getting anxious. They want to know if they should be getting ready for us.'

'Well, don't worry about it. We'll go another day.'

After a few more words – quite a few, and not all of them civil – Ismael and I got in the pickup, put the driver in the back and headed to Addis Ababa. When we arrived, Ismael asked Solomon, one of our Addis staff, if he'd got a ticket for us.

'Not exactly, but I've shopped around and found the cheapest – Yemeni Airlines. You can go any day you like.'

I thought that was a bit strange, as flights going to Australia are usually booked weeks in advance. Ismael, though, loves a bargain. He told Solomon to buy the tickets.

A few days later we boarded a very tired-looking aeroplane

bound for Sanaa, the capital of Yemen. The seats sagged and were torn in places, the carpet was threadbare. Everything looked old and worn. This plane had done a lot of miles. Even Aisha thought it looked a bit run-down. Still, it flew. From Sanaa we went on to Dubai, where we were due to change to an Air India flight to Bombay, then Sydney.

At Dubai we approached the Air India counter and presented our tickets. The booking clerk poked at his computer and gave us an apologetic look. 'You're not on the flight.'

'There must be a mistake. Please, have another look.'

He did, with the same result. Then he examined our tickets more closely. 'Ah, Yemeni Airlines. They do this all the time. They've stranded people all over the world. And this flight is fully booked.'

I said, 'Can you book us on another airline?'

'It's not as easy as that. We have to sell this ticket to another airline and try to book you through.'

I put through a reverse-charge call to David and told him there was a bit of a hitch. He was in the midst of organising a surprise party with all the relatives.

We spent the next two days at Dubai airport trying to find a flight to Australia. At night we slept on the airport benches. It was Bangkok all over again. At one stage Ismael decided he'd like to visit the airport mosque. It features a huge wall of glass, which Ismael walked right into, sending Aisha into a fit of laughter and leaving poor Ismael with a badly bruised face.

On the third day I reckoned it was time for desperate measures. I saw the airport manager and explained our situation. 'I can't do this,' I told him. 'This child is driving me crazy trying to keep her amused. I've got to get out of here.'

He was a kind man. He arranged for us to stay at the airport hotel, where we were able to have proper showers and eat some real food, not just takeaway snacks.

Next day we were booked on a flight to Hong Kong. Shortly before we were due to board I thought I'd tidy up my handbag. I emptied all the accumulated receipts and ticket stubs and rubbish into the bin. We joined the queue waiting to get on the plane. When we got to the counter to present our boarding passes I couldn't find them.

'Oh, Mumma, how could you,' wailed Aisha, no doubt picturing more interminable days in Dubai airport. The man at the gate was unsympathetic. No boarding passes, no boarding. I racked my brains. Had I left them in the washroom? Had I dropped them when I'd paid for that sandwich at the snack bar? The rubbish bin? I said to Ismael, 'This is going to be embarrassing but I'm going to have to empty that rubbish bin.'

'Okay, let's do it.'

Under the disapproving gazes of scores of passengers, I upended the bin onto the floor, and there . . . well . . . I don't have to tell you the rest of the story.

This wasn't the last time we had dramas of this kind. Somehow, international travel never goes smoothly for me.

After Aisha had been born, we'd tried without success to have more children. I presume that my age plus Aisha's traumatic birth were the problem. We tried fertility treatment but after five or six years I had to resign myself to the fact that I couldn't have any more children.

I asked Ismael what he thought about adoption. Initially he was against it, but after a while he came to think that it was a good idea. A couple of years passed and he did nothing about it. One day when I was in Addis by myself, I thought, why don't I look into it? Ismael's never going to get around to it.

I asked Solomon if he knew anything about the orphanages around town. 'There are lots of them,' he said.

'Yes, but do you know any specifically?'

'Well, there's one place at the top of the piazza, Abenich Gorbena.'

I asked him to take me there, but not to leave me, as I'd need him to do the Amharic translation. All I wanted to know were the requirements for adoption, so I'd know whether we fitted the guidelines or not. I thought if we were suitable, I might take away some forms for Ismael and me to fill in.

We arrived at the orphanage, in an old part of Addis at the end of a rutted road. Abenich Gorbena had been founded many years ago by an Ethiopian woman, and was still run by Ethiopians. We passed through a pair of big steel gates to a ramshackle old house with wide verandahs. It must have been very grand once but it was a bit run-down looking now. There were 140 children living in the orphanage, ranging from babies, to teenagers who were going to school or learning trades.

There were children everywhere. The rooms had bunk beds, and in some of them the children were sleeping two or three to a bed. A very nice, motherly woman who was showing us around told us that they liked it like that. It made them feel part of a big family.

It was bathing time. Some had already had their baths and were getting dressed. They came running up to us, grasping us around the legs. Some demanded, *'Earsas sichini'* – give me a pencil. Others tried out their English with 'What is your name?'

Solomon explained to our guide who I was and what I wanted. She said to him, 'Well, she'd better choose a baby.'

He translated and I replied, 'No, I don't want to choose one. Number one, my husband's not here and, number two, I might choose a dress in a shop like that but not a baby. I just want to know your procedures. Do we need an interview, who do we have to see? That sort of thing.'

At this stage Solomon remembered he had to go to attend

night school. I still hadn't found out what I wanted to know, so it seemed I'd just have to muddle along without him. Solomon left, and the woman seized me by the arm and led me into the baby section. There were three babies lying in cots. One was standing up, rattling the sides of the cot. He was a bit more than a year old. He had just come in and had not yet been processed.

In another cot there were two babies together. One was a very pretty little girl with a fine head of thick, black hair. They said she was named Borlice because the police had brought her in.

The other baby was lying on his back kicking his legs. 'What about this little fellow?' I said.

'Oh, nobody's interested in that one.'

'I might be interested.'

'Okay, that one, then. Pick him up.'

I did as she suggested. I put him on my shoulder, and he reached his arm around my neck and gave me a firm cuddle. I thought to myself, this is a nice little boy. I like him.

The woman in charge told me that he'd been left in a basket at the door of the orphanage. He must have been born very recently as the umbilical cord had still been attached. It usually falls off after three or four days. I asked if I could visit him. I think she was disappointed that I didn't sign up then. A lot of foreigners come to Ethiopia looking for children because this is one of the easiest places in the world to adopt. In the last five years they had adopted over 100 children to foreign parents but only five to Ethiopians. I think she was very keen that we, as Ethiopian parents, should succeed. She said, yes, visiting would be all right.

I left the orphanage with my mind in a whirl. What would Ismael think? What would my family think? If they utterly disapproved, would it be selfish of me to do this? Was I really ready for another child when I never had enough time to spend with the one I already had? I wished I could turn to my mother for advice, or my sisters who all had two or three children. I'd told Pauline that I was thinking of adoption and she'd advised me to think really carefully. I badly needed their confirmation.

The closest person to family I had in Addis Ababa was Stephanie, the wife of my nephew, Andrew Browning. Andrew was an obstetrician working at the Fistula Hospital, with Dr Catherine Hamlin.

I took Stephanie back to the orphanage for a visit. Ismael refused to go, saying, 'I don't go into such places. I don't like that sort of idea.' In Afar society, you don't find orphans, they're looked after by the extended family.

Stephanie lifted the baby out of the cot and declared, 'He's a living angel. So peaceful and beautiful. The family would love him.'

The process took four months. When all the formalities had been completed, Ismael asked his friend Ilyas to go with me to fetch our new son and to drive us home. I asked Ismael, 'What about you?'

'What do you need me for?' he said.

The baby was very thin – malnourished, really – and they told me he was constipated, which is hardly possible for a tiny baby. The problem was he'd been lying in his cot for eight months with a bottle of half powdered milk and half water in his mouth. His left eye had two spots indicating vitamin A deficiency. He was so weak that he couldn't even sit up and control his head.

In all that time he'd had no stimulation – no lights, no noise, no music, nothing, he'd just been lying there. Sitting on my knee in the car, his little eyes were swivelling everywhere, from the radio, to the movement outside, to Ilyas and to me. When we got him home I gave him baby food mixed with avocados. He ate voraciously and he has done ever since.

We called him Rammidos – which means 'root', as in 'root of

humanity'. From the moment he set eyes on him, Ismael loved him dearly.

As I write, Rammid is six years old. Where he got his genetic makeup from, nobody knows. From the moment he could walk, he was a wild little boy. When he was three years old, the four of us made another trip to Australia, this time via South Africa. We had a nine-hour wait in Johannesburg before catching the flight to Melbourne. Rammid did not stop running around in all that time. He was in and out of the shops, tearing things off the shelves and generally creating havoc. If one of us turned away for a moment, he would instantly disappear into the crowd.

Once, a line of people was boarding a flight. Rammid spied a key slipped into the side pocket of a man's bag. He grabbed it and ran into the crowd. I chased him and got the key, but then I couldn't remember which passenger he'd taken it from. After searching for some minutes, I thought I recognised the bag. I sheepishly asked its owner if he had lost his key. He had, and he was not amused.

On the plane Rammid could not keep still. The only thing that made him content was when he was out of the seat on the floor putting things in and out of my shoes. The Qantas staff wouldn't allow that and insisted that he remain in his seat. The result was that the trip was very trying for us and, I'm sure, for the nearby passengers.

We had planned to stay with my mother in Australia. But Rammid was so hyperactive that we moved to a place Rowene had bought in nearby Mittagong.

David was so concerned about Rammid's behaviour that he asked a paediatrician friend to have a look at him. He diagnosed Attention Deficit Hyperactivity Disorder and recommended that we put him on the drug Ritalin.

I don't believe in dosing up children. Rammid lives with Ismael and me in our compound, and goes to a local school. He speaks Amharic and Afar, and his English is coming along. He's not performing all that well in school. He's behind in his reading and writing, but he mentally recalls everything they tell him. I believe that basically he's a brilliant child, and that's the problem. I suspect he's going to be bored with the classroom and I don't know what we'll do about that. He shows an intense interest in everything to do with cars. He can start one up, which is a worry, and he loves to talk to the drivers and be with them when they're working on the engines and changing wheels and so on. He asks lots of questions. I think he's developing okay. We can't do anything about the ADHD. Here, we accept all children as they are. I'm sure he'll turn out just fine in the end. He's been an incredible son to Ismael and me, and an absolute bonus, considering I can't have any more children. Right from the beginning, he's been a loving little boy. I just wish I had more time to spend with him. I treasure the rare quiet moments we have together when he curls up in my lap at the end of the day for a bit of a chat and a cuddle. Little Rammid. Precious beyond price.

CHAPTER 18

Ever since the government investigation, official attitudes towards APDA had changed for the better. From 2001 the government of the Afar region started to acknowledge us. I was invited to meet the state president, who went out of his way to be nice to me – once calling me his sister-in-law! The central government began asking Ismael to attend meetings in Addis Ababa because of his special knowledge of Afar. The government's policy was to try to accommodate Afar culture in education, law and health. In practice, it was, and is, hard to make this work. Most civil servants are still Amharic-speaking highlanders and, until education becomes widespread in the Afar region, it's likely to remain that way.

APDA depends mainly on funds donated by NGOs and aid agencies. We work in tandem with the government on certain projects. This is often frustrating, as we can do things faster, cheaper and more efficiently than they can. Vaccination programs are a typical example.

In late 2002 I began receiving reports from our health workers in remote parts of the Dubte area that people were dying of measles. We informed the health department and, in due course, they told us that they'd carried out a vaccination program.

Still, reports of deaths kept coming in. People were dying of measles, whooping cough, things that we could have prevented. I had a pretty good idea what had happened with the vaccination program because I'd seen it before. Someone in an office somewhere makes up a plan on computer about how many vaccinations they're going to do, and allocates a certain time for the job – say, a week. The administration office dishes out the money. There will probably be a few arguments about how it's going to be divided up, which takes a couple of days, so they've got five days left to do the job. Vaccines have to be kept refrigerated. The government workers collect their ice in some regional centre like Dessie or Dubte, which might be 400 kilometres away from where they're working. Then they drive as close as they can to the vaccination area. They might still have to walk for 24 hours to get there. Most government workers won't walk, they want to be driven, but they can't be because there are no roads. By the time all this has been sorted out, the ice has melted anyway and the vaccines have been ruined.

Sometimes the government workers just dig a hole and bury the vaccines, then sign the forms to say they've achieved 90 per cent coverage. I know. I've found them. When it happened, I told UNICEF, who'd funded the program. They said they thought that might have been the case. I said it was obvious, because this area that was supposed to have huge measles vaccination coverage had had a measles outbreak. Still they persist in giving vaccination money to the government.

When I heard that the government program had failed, I pestered them to allow us to do the job. At first they wouldn't acknowledge that there was a problem. It's not in my nature to give up when people's lives are at stake; opposition just makes me more determined. I ended up going down to Addis Ababa and pounding on doors all over town until someone listened to me. The central government sent an expert from the capital to assess the situation and found, as I'd been telling them, that very little vaccinating had been done.

They gave us the funds for a program covering the full range of childhood diseases, plus tetanus, and enough funds to keep our health workers in the field for seven days. They chose that amount of time because they pay workers by the week, and seven days fits nicely into the plan they've devised on computer. Rashly, we agreed.

It took us seven weeks – seven weeks working in some of the harshest country on the planet.

Our vaccination method is to take a refrigerator, and a generator to run it, on a truck as far into the area as possible. We set up base near a water source, load the vaccines into ice chests and use camels donated by the community to carry them into the wilderness. When the vaccines have been used, the camels return to base and pick up another load. A boy stays with the generator and ice chest under a tree, filling up plastic bags with water and freezing them so they're ready to send out with each foray.

We had agreed with the government to do all the hard-to-reach areas. I had to put every single health worker I could muster into the campaign, about 75 people all told. They were all highly motivated Afar. No one else would work as hard as they did. We travelled hundreds of kilometres on foot – no one knows how many – sometimes running with camels by the light of the moon to get to a location before the ice melted.

We used the government funds to buy sugar, white flour to cook *ga'ambo*, tea, *shiro*, and plenty of coffee – the men have to have their coffee to keep going. When we were short on time, I fed them with ground barley, sugar and water. I'd get them to drink it fast and urge them to get going again. I gave them the sugar to keep their energy levels up.

We were going into areas the government had never reached. I don't know how many people we vaccinated, but it's not the count so much as the coverage which is important. We reckoned we achieved something like 93 or 94 per cent. We chased down every single child. If we found that the child had gone away with the goats, we'd wait for that child to return. It was the most nightmarish trip I think I've ever done. We all lost kilos in weight and I had to replace some workers who just couldn't take it.

The government aren't able to do this sort of work. It's not in their guidelines. Their protocols are drawn up for the town where people take their children to a clinic. In the desert, people have never heard of vaccination to begin with. You've got to persuade them that it's not dangerous. They reason that if a person isn't sick, why give them a needle? They sometimes think we're injecting women because we don't want them to have any more children. We have to tell them that this vaccine is used all over the world and it's simply for their protection.

This program was a classic example of why you should involve community effort. It's good that governments and inter-national aid agencies contribute, but they should keep their hands off the implementation. If they demand that you do things the way they've been worked out in Geneva, or Addis Ababa, it just won't work. The Afar are a unique society living in a killer environment. If you don't use their local knowledge, you often end up simply entering into a computer data which bears no relation to what's really happened on the ground. The well-meaning agency will think they've given this money and they've achieved so much coverage according to the age grouping and so on; they've drawn up graphs and maps in lovely colours, but it's nonsense. They're just bits of paper, as far as I'm concerned.

*

Shortly after we finished that program, we moved from Assaita 57 kilometres away to the headquarters we now occupy in Logia. Everyone was reluctant to leave Assaita beside the beautiful Awash River for this dust-blown little town on the main truck route between Addis and Djibouti. We did it because the regional government had moved their headquarters to nearby Samara and, as much as possible, we try to work with them.

One day in late September, not long after we'd returned home from visiting Mother, Rosemary rang from Australia. The housegirl answered the phone. Rosemary wanted to know where I was. 'She's on a trip,' was the reply.

'What does that mean? Is she one day away, three days, a week or what?'

The housegirl didn't know and Rosemary hung up, not knowing when she'd be able to get in touch.

As luck would have it, I arrived back that night and heard that Rosemary wanted to speak to me urgently. I suspected what it was about before I rang back. While we'd been in Australia, I'd learned that Mother had cancer. No one had noticed that she was unwell, as she never complained about anything. She'd gone to the supermarket and bought a load of groceries. She asked the man on the counter to deliver it. He said, 'Why, Mrs Browning, you never have things delivered. Aren't you feeling well?'

'I'm feeling a bit tired today. Do you think you could spoil me for once?'

'Of course, Mrs Browning, but if you're feeling a bit tired does that mean you need a checkup by the doctor?'

Her GP ordered a CT scan of her abdomen. They found an enormous pancreatic cancer that had already grown over to her stomach.

Even then, she never let on that she was in trouble. She told the neighbours that she wouldn't be around with strawberries from the garden for a while. 'But I'll pick up,' she assured them. 'I'll be around as soon as I feel well again.'

She was in great pain and vomiting bile. Her bile duct became completely blocked and she had to go to Liverpool hospital to have a stent put in to drain it. I think she knew then she was dying. She prepared for her death with the thoughtfulness that had characterised her whole life. She cleaned the curtains in the house, made up a lot of little packages with gifts for various people, of things she wouldn't need anymore, or else things that they might have once told her they liked.

Rosemary's phone call confirmed my worst fears. 'If you want to see her,' advised Rosemary, 'you'd better come as quick as you can.'

I hadn't been home for my father's death and it had taken me a long time to accept that. Now it looked as if I would not be there for Mother either. Ismael said of course I must go; the trouble was, we could not afford a plane ticket. I was in despair until one of our workers, dear old Waasi, The Cowboy, offered me the money. I refused at first – it was an enormous amount of money for an Afar – but Waasi insisted and in the end my craving to see my mother before she died won out.

In early November I boarded a plane for the long flight to Melbourne and then the train trip to Moss Vale. When I arrived I went straight to Mother's house. My brothers had been constantly phoning and visiting, while my sisters were taking it in turns to be with her around the clock. It was Rosemary who looked up and saw me flit past the kitchen window. She was thrilled because now the family was complete and Mother could die content.

Mother was sitting in a chair when I walked in. In fact, it wasn't until the last 24 hours of her life that she was completely bedridden. She said to me, 'Look, dear, they've made me rattle. Can you hear all that rattling in my stomach?'

She was taking Panadeine three times a day. She would only ever take one at a time. I said to her, 'Use five packets a day if you want, I don't mind, we want you to be comfortable.'

'No, dear, it's embarrassing. There are visitors coming and I'm rattling like an empty barrel.'

It was only afterwards that I learned from her GP that she'd been in great pain. The surgeon who put in the stent to drain her bile duct had telephoned him afterwards and chastised him for leaving her so long without pain treatment. He could only plead ignorance. She'd been so stoic about it that he never even knew.

Over the following eight days Mother taught us how to depart this life in a very peaceful way – accepting of death and appreciating the life she'd lived. She spoke to us each in turn. I treasure that time – having been able to sit quietly with her, reminiscing about our lives together, telling her about her grandchildren, Aisha and Rammid, sometimes just silently holding her hand.

In her final 24 hours she called us all in one by one for a little talk. She had a cheery word for each of us. Then we all gathered around her bed for her final moments.

My mother had led an exemplary life. She had taught me many good lessons. She always said that the best thing in life is contentment, because if you aspire to a life you haven't got, then you make yourself miserable over nothing. She'd never had luxuries, yet she was always happy. She loved her husband and family, and took pleasure in their achievements. She enjoyed simple things such as gardening, making jam and giving it away to people, going shopping for others; she was quite happy with that. She never approved of sitting down and complaining. 'You've got to get on with things,' she'd say. I've written down everything about those last precious days with her and I hope I've learned something. She'd always supported me without question and now, at the age of 87, she was gone. I miss her more than I can say.

CHAPTER 19

When we first moved to Logia, we lived on the verandah of a house owned by one of APDA's workers, Kamil. After a couple of years another of our workers, Kalil, said to Ismael, 'You and Maalika have nothing to call a home. I'll put in a bit of money and you put in some, and why don't you buy something?'

So, with the help of Kalil and some others, we bought the little house in the compound in Logia where we now live. We then added a long wing of extra rooms. It looks atrocious. I didn't see it until it was built; I would never have agreed to something that looks like a row of concrete cells. The compound now consists of three low buildings in an L shape. The half a dozen rooms on the long side of the L are always occupied by Afar who are in need of help. They might be refugees from Eritrea, or people with serious illnesses requiring treatment, or just people down on their luck. There's never enough shelter for them all, so we keep a supply of straw mats for some to sleep on outside. One of the rooms is a storeroom where we keep sacks of pasta, lentils, chickpeas and flour to feed them all.

The short side of the L is made up of two small rooms; again, of concrete. One is where Ismael, Rammid and I sleep. It's about

5 metres square, with a door and no windows. Inside are two iron-frame beds, a cupboard, a chest of drawers, a couple of stools – that's it for furniture. The floor is covered in linoleum which is torn and coming up in places; there's a ceiling fan, and a single bare light bulb. The walls are decorated with half a dozen pictures of African animals cut out of a magazine. In one corner is a TV set, which is connected to a satellite dish. Ismael is a news junkie and likes to watch Al Jazeera or BBC World News.

Next to our room is a kitchen with a refrigerator and a table for preparing food. In practice, all food is cooked over an open fire in a traditional stick-and-mud hut which sits apart from the other buildings.

The third building consists of two concrete cubicles containing the toilet and a cold-water shower. These facilities are shared by everyone.

My dream is to build a kindergarten and school in the compound, and put up a *deboita* with lots of Afar things in there so that the town Afar can learn about their culture.

If I'm not away on a trip, I get up just before dawn and spend a few minutes reading my Bible. Ismael, meanwhile, will be performing his devotions on his prayer mat. I never eat much – just a few mouthfuls of *ga'ambo* and lentils and a cup of sweet *shahi*. By the time the sun is beginning to lift above the horizon, I say goodbye to Rammid and head off either with Ismael or by myself to APDA's administration offices.

My route takes me along a series of dirt pathways which wind between mud-and-stick houses. As I go along, I can observe the rest of the town starting their day. Families are squatting in their yards eating breakfast; children are leaving for school; someone might be looking for a goat – they wander about the streets at will but everyone knows who owns which animal; an occasional horse-drawn cart will come by with passengers going off to the market. Usually if a white person ventures into this part of town, the children will taunt them with, *'Ferengi, ferengi,'* – foreigner – and sometimes ask for money. But they know me, and give me a polite greeting or else leave me alone.

It's about a ten-minute walk to the administration compound, where we have offices, storerooms for medicines and school supplies, a meeting room and a yard where we keep the vehicles. My 'office' is a desk in a corner of the meeting room. There's a phone and fax available, but emails have to be faxed to our office in Addis Ababa, which copies them out and sends them. To reply, the same thing happens in reverse. Communications are not exactly speedy.

There are never enough hours in the day to do everything. On a short day, I'll get home at about seven thirty or eight o'clock. Often it's later than that. I was asked recently what I'd do if I had a holiday. I answered that I'd love to catch up on a few years' sleep. The truth is that I really don't know what I'd do. Going to a resort and sitting around on a deck chair reading books just doesn't make any sense to me. My problem is that I can't relax. I know this is not good. I know my working habits are bad for my husband and for my children, but I can't slow down. There's too much to be done.

I'm all too aware that my children are suffering for this work. Whenever I'm about to leave on a trip, Rammid goes out to the vehicle and sits in the passenger seat. He looks at me with his beautiful brown eyes and pleads, 'Will you take me with you? If you take me, I won't play up; I'll be a good boy, I'll be so nice, I promise you.'

I have to tell him, 'Oh, Rammid, even if you're a good boy, I can't take you.'

He gets out and watches with tears in his eyes as I drive away. It's horrible to see him crying. I hate leaving my children, but then, that's the choice I must face. Do I sacrifice the work or my children? I'm not living a normal mother's life, with a nice kitchen and house and all that. Some people get those things and some don't. I guess it just wasn't the hand I was dealt.

I've had screaming matches with God when I've cried, 'Let me out of this. You know me, you forget my nationality, I'm not supposed to be here, my time is up.' Every time, I get pulled back, and I'm reminded that this is what I'm meant to be doing.

As I write this, Rammid is six and Aisha is sixteen. Aisha lives in our rented two-bedroom flat in Addis Ababa. It seems as if I've *always* been too busy to give her the time she deserves. Even when she was a little baby and I had to take her to work with me in Djibouti, if I was too busy to pick her up, I'd turn on a cassette player and she'd lie there waving her hands in time to the music while she waited for attention.

Aisha's a city girl at heart. She knows all the international pop stars and, at the same time, loves Afar and Indian music. She can listen to her MP3 player for hours. She likes to watch Bollywood movies on TV with her girlfriends, as well as Egyptian soapies and American shows, such as *Oprah*, on our satellite TV. She makes no bones about the fact that she doesn't like Logia; she prefers to be with her friends in the bright lights of Addis. She's crazy about fashion, and she's in despair about my lack of interest in clothes. She told me a while ago, 'Mummy, you have no style.'

'What do you mean?'

'You're supposed to wiggle your bottom when you walk.'

'I don't know if you've noticed, my dear, that I don't have a bottom.'

Either Ismael or I get down to Addis to see her about once every month or six weeks. Our housegirl has strict instructions that she has to sleep in Aisha's room with her, as there are always Afar men camping on the floor of the lounge room. Not that I expect trouble, but Aisha is a beautiful girl and it's best to be careful.

In school holidays she comes up to Logia to stay. But even then she hardly sees us. I'm either working from dawn till dusk in the office or else away in the desert, while Ismael puts in the same sort of hours as well.

There are usually one or two children staying in the compound for Rammid to play with. There are two or three Eritrean boys of about Aisha's age at the compound, who we are putting through school. They are company for her but she'd really rather be gossiping with her girlfriends.

Once when I was in Logia and Ismael was in Addis, Aisha telephoned me in tears. 'Mummy,' she said, 'Daddy's gone out and there's no money in the house to buy bread.'

Ismael had forgotten to leave any, so Aisha had no breakfast that day. Another time, when she was eleven, we were having an argument about her wanting a day off school. I was insisting that she went. In anger, she said, 'Why should I go to school? There's no mother or father around here, anyway. What's the point?'

I've cried many times for Aisha. The amazing thing is that she has managed to grow into a delightful, fun-loving, well-adjusted young woman who is in love with life. She's not rebellious or petulant like some of the western teenagers I've met. She looks adults in the eye and can converse easily with them in three different languages. Once, a well-meaning grown-up asked her who looked after her when Mummy and Daddy were away. She answered, 'Me, my nanny and God.'

Aisha goes to an international school with children from many different countries. I'm often asked why I didn't send Aisha to Australia to be educated; there are plenty of family members who'd have been happy to look after her. However, I'm not impressed with the way western children are brought up. I fear that Aisha would lose the traditional values of modesty and respect. I also don't like the competitiveness of the educational system. If she went to Australia as a schoolgirl, she'd lose her Ethiopian values and I doubt she'd ever get them back. She'd always think of Ethiopia as 'poor' in a negative way and not understand it. It will be different when she's of university age. She'll be more mature and less vulnerable. She may well go to Australia for further study when she finishes school here. She doesn't know what she wants to do yet – one day she says she'll be a movie star and the next she wants to do nursing. She's sure of one thing – as much as she's proud to be Afar, she has no desire to spend her life in a dust-blown little town in northern Ethiopia running a struggling NGO.

I'm always aware that the health risks for children are greater here than in the developed world. When Aisha was four, she caught hepatitis. A western doctor will tell you there's no cure for the disease. They usually prescribe rest, lots of sweet fluids and vitamin B. But Aisha *was* cured, by traditional Afar medicine.

She was very, very sick. Her skin was yellow, she had low-grade fever, was lethargic and weepy, sitting on my knee, clinging to me and not wanting to eat or play. We were in Addis Ababa at the time. Some Afar in Logia heard about it and told me, 'Believe us, Maalika, we can cure her.'

I was very nervous. She was a little girl and she seemed to be falling apart before my eyes. There was no point contacting my brothers or sisters or aunt and asking them to help; they were in Australia. I couldn't take Aisha there because there wasn't time or the money for the fares. I didn't even have enough money to go to a local doctor. It came down to what options we *did* have right here.

I saw that Aisha's life was not in my hands as it would be in a European society. I had to think that maybe the Afar way was right and go for it – that, and pray. The average western person rejects the spiritual side of life. They think that it's nonsense because it's not tangible – you can't touch it. But to deny the spirit is to deny your own being. When you pray to God, you're not making a request like a shopping list. You're submitting to His will. You are saying in prayer, 'I believe, God, that you know what's best for Aisha.' Even if God chose that she died, I couldn't say that would be the worst outcome. It would be God's will.

Ismael said there was no question that we had to treat her – we couldn't leave her the way she was. The elders in Logia sent us a piece of bark and a root from the Waybala tree, which is a sort of acacia. You grind it up, soak it in water and she had to drink it for seven days. I had to force her to take it, as it tastes very bitter.

On the third day, she had a massive diuresis. She couldn't stop passing urine. I could see the jaundice colour draining out of her body. On the following day, she was a different person, playing and asking for food.

When she was six, Aisha contracted cerebral malaria. This wicked disease is a real killer. If left untreated, a patient can die within 24 to 72 hours. Even with treatment, 15 per cent of children and 20 per cent of adults with cerebral malaria die.

We were living in Assaita at the time. Aisha woke up in the morning feeling unwell. She got out of bed but when she went to have her breakfast, she felt dizzy. She went back to bed again and that's the last thing she remembers.

I was thinking I should give her some aspirin, when one of our staff came running, saying that Aisha was convulsing. I knew straight away what it was. I rushed to a government health worker I knew in town and got him to bring quinine. It was an hour before she stopped convulsing.

It was this quick treatment that saved Aisha's life. A few years later, one of her closest friends was not so fortunate. Bob and Sonja Hedley and their two daughters, Bronwen and Rosanna, were good friends of ours. Bob, who's Dutch, works for an international NGO and travels quite a bit in remote parts of Ethiopia. The family had spent some time in the Awash National Park sleeping out without mosquito nets.

I was in Addis Ababa when it happened. Bronwen called me to say that her sister was in hospital with cerebral malaria, her father was behaving strangely and her mother didn't know what to do. I rushed over to their place immediately. Bob was incoherent and had terrible diarrhoea. He didn't seem to know where he was or what he was doing. Irrational behaviour is one of the symptoms of cerebral malaria. The parasite attacks the red blood cells, and the blood vessels in the brain become blocked, causing you to convulse. It also attacks the kidneys and stops them working. I was pretty sure that Bob also had cerebral malaria. We needed to get him to hospital quickly.

We took him by taxi to the same private hospital where Rosanna was. By the time we got there, poor Bob was raving like a madman. He wouldn't allow anyone to wash him except me. When that was done I had a battle getting him into bed.

He settled at last and I went to see how Rosanna was getting on. She was a lot sicker than her father. She was lying in bed in a ward with other patients. I could see that she was haemolysing – that is, her red blood cells were breaking down – as she was turning white in front of our eyes. I looked at her chart. The staff had only given her one dose of quinine and I knew she should have had more. She should have had a loading dose. The quinine has to get to a certain level in the blood to stop the blockage to the brain. She'd have been much better off in the Black Lion hospital, which is a public hospital and used to dealing with cerebral malaria. The staff didn't agree with me about the quinine dosage. When I suggested taking Rosanna to the Black

Lion they waved me away, telling me not to worry, that it was in their hands. I then insisted that they transfer her to an intensive care ward, which they reluctantly agreed to do.

Patients with cerebral malaria need to be closely monitored. I was worried that they wouldn't do it – with good cause, as it turned out. In the middle of the night I looked in on her and there was not a soul there. The nurses were all asleep – in fact, they'd brought their night clothes and slippers to work with them!

Rosanna looked terrible. Her skin was deathly white, tinged with yellow, and she was drifting in and out of consciousness. Blood was all over the floor. In a fury I woke one of the nurses and demanded that she call the doctor.

He was also asleep – and not happy about being woken, either. I had no confidence in his ability, or even his willingness, to treat Rosanna properly. I said I wanted to give blood so that she could have a transfusion. He wouldn't agree that it was necessary. After badgering him, he at last gave me the papers I needed to take to the Red Cross to give the blood. When I returned to the hospital, they gave her the blood unit and then she vomited once more. I offered to go again. The doctor told me, 'Don't be ridiculous, this is an overload.'

Blood was all over the floor. She had vomited huge amounts. I said, 'I'll bring any number of donors. I can wake up people. I can bring money, anything, but please act.'

'No, no,' he said. 'We're in control here, you're not. Don't wake me up again.' Then he slammed the door to intensive care in my face.

When I'd first arrived I'd asked Sonja for the contact details of a doctor she knew who worked with Médecins sans Frontières. I thought he would be able to organise a medical evacuation. In her distressed state she'd been unable to comprehend what I wanted. Now, at last, she gave me his number. I called him and straight away he ordered a medically equipped aeroplane from Geneva.

I don't know how many hours later it arrived in Addis Ababa – too many. The doctor who was meant to be treating Rosanna was so furious at losing his patient that he and his staff refused to help load her onto the ambulance.

On the plane they had a dialysis machine, they intubated her, they did everything they had not been doing at the hospital. Sonja flew with Rosanna to Nairobi, where she was placed in hospital in intensive care. By then she was in a coma and on life support. Bronwen stayed behind with her dad.

I'd been up for well over 24 hours by the time they took off, without food or even taking time to go to the toilet. I staggered home and, as soon as I sat down, was seized by nausea. I vomited and vomited until I couldn't anymore, and then I slept the sleep of utter exhaustion.

I had little hope that poor Rosanna would survive. A few days later, Bob, by no means fit, but well enough to leave hospital, flew with Bronwen to Nairobi. There, they had to make the most awful decision that any family could face. A week after Rosanna had arrived, the life support equipment was turned off.

Rosanna was twelve, two years older than Aisha. They'd been very close. While she had still been conscious, Aisha had spoken to her on the telephone. She told Rosanna that she was going to get well and that they'd ride horses together. That had been their big dream. Aisha was brokenhearted at her loss. She's told me that she'd never had a friend like Rosanna and she doesn't think she ever will have again. She can't understand why God would take a vibrant young girl with her whole life ahead of her. For me, the worst of it was that if Rosanna had received proper care from the beginning, she could have lived.

*

Rosanna's death was symptomatic of what's wrong with the hospital system in Ethiopia. Western standards of cleanliness and ethical practice are unheard of. I once took a woman to one of the government hospitals in the Afar region to give birth. In the delivery room, the placenta from the previous patient was still there in a bowl on the table. This was the table I was supposed to put my patient on. There was a sickly smell in the room. I asked a nurse to take the placenta away. She refused. 'That's not my job,' she said.

'Whose job is it, then?'

'The cleaner's.'

I said, 'You're a nurse, my dear, let's get rid of it. Where can we throw this stuff? I don't want my patient to see it. It'll frighten her.'

I'd love to close that hospital. Their idea of hygiene and management is unbelievable. I've taken HIV patients there who have been far down the track of AIDS and they've refused them antiretroviral medicine.

The first time it happened, I asked, 'What's your criterion for selection?'

'That's our business.'

I said, 'I'm not moving. I'm going to stand here until you admit this man for treatment. What do you think of that?'

Sometimes the only way to get them to act is to bully them. I can do it, but it's asking a great deal for an Afar pastoralist straight out of the desert to stand up for his or her rights.

With our health workers, traditional birth attendants and women's extension workers, APDA now has its own system of primary health care, but there's a gap in that system. We want to lower the maternal death rate, but once we find a woman in trouble, the big question is where to refer her. The two government hospitals are not run by Afar. There are a few there, but only very few. It's not the Afar mentality that governs the hospital, and the patients we send can simply be refused treatment if hospital officials want to.

A friend's wife was turned away and she died on the road seeking medical help. She had delivered her fifth baby. Worried about her condition, her relatives managed to borrow a vehicle and take her and the baby to the hospital. The hospital should have realised that she was so anaemic she needed a blood transfusion. With the relatives present, there would have been no trouble obtaining blood. Instead, she was told to go away. They then headed for the only other hospital in Afar. I found them broken down on the road. My driver helped them get started but, before they could get to the hospital, she died.

APDA has plans to build our own women's hospital. It will be for training, prevention and treatment of obstetric problems. For instance, there are thousands of Afar women with prolapsed uteruses, which is a horrible affliction to live with. We want something that is very ethically grounded, with good professional standards of treatment. At first, we'll have western obstetricians and midwives as the teachers and frontline treaters. They'll slowly step back as the Afar become more skilled. My brother David, who's retired from his obstetrics work, says there would be plenty of people like him who'd be glad to give a few months' voluntary service. My nephew Andrew is also an obstetrician. He runs an outreach of the Fistula Hospital at Bahar Dar in northern Ethiopia. He's had some architect friends in Australia draw up plans for a simple little hospital of 28 beds. They did the job gratis. On his last trip home, he raised $100,000 from a church in Broken Hill, where he once lived. A merchant banker friend of his contributed $60,000 from his annual bonus. (It makes me wonder what his salary is!) That should be enough to get us started. Of course, it's a project that will need continuing support for running costs.

We'll site the hospital at Mille, which is a central position with good access roads and a catchment of about half a million people. In the future, we could have our own health clinics up and down the main trade road, where women can go when they're coming to term. They'll have waiting areas with health officers who can assess whether or not they'll be at risk delivering. The high-risk ones will go to the hospital to have their babies and the low-risk ones will deliver in the health clinics. If there's a problem, they can hop in the car and be at the hospital in an hour or two.

CHAPTER 20

When I look back over the last fifteen years, I'm amazed at how APDA has grown, from that first meeting of clan leaders at Sidiica Mangela, with all of our tentative hopes and dreams, to an organisation employing more than 550 people. For the first three years, we scraped by on the salary that I'd saved from working as a nurse in Djibouti. At about the time that money was due to run out, I had delivered one of our 'Updates' to the head of Oxfam in Addis Ababa, Colin Mason. I mentioned that we were probably going to have to give up on our dream of being a local NGO. He was shocked. 'You can't do that,' he said, 'you've got to do something. You can't go back.'

'We'll have to,' I said. 'We've done it all on our own so far and now the money's dried up.'

I described to him how we'd been operating – the camel trips into Djibouti, the constant fear of capture by the Issa army, the daily sacrifices our Afar colleagues were making to help their countrymen. I suspect it was when I told him about Ahmed Ali Angaddu starving to death that Colin made up his mind to help us. He offered to give us an administration budget. I had to calculate all our expenses – how many stamps we needed for a year, how much for fares to ride on trucks from Addis to Bure, a tiny budget for telephone calls. The total came to a minuscule amount. But it saved us from going under.

Oxfam's involvement had continued the following year with backing for primary health and education for Afar near the Eritrean border. They continued to help us until war broke out in 1998, then Oxfam Great Britain had what they called a 'change in strategic direction'. They decided they'd no longer do hands-on development, education and health. Instead, they were going to do 'capacity building', lobbying and advocacy. In other words, jump from real hands-on work to the airy-fairy stuff.

I asked them what this meant for APDA. There was a simple answer – they were cancelling our project.

I said, 'You can't do that. Not now. War's broken out. The community woke up yesterday to find that there were thousands of military personnel in their area with tanks and rocket launchers and artillery. The women are afraid to go out and tend their goats; they can't market their animals because they're not permitted to move by the military, they don't know what to do with themselves. These people need more help, not less. You can't just tell them, "We've had a nice time together – now, bye bye, look after your own health and education."'

It made no difference. I drafted a letter to Oxfam in London threatening to expose them through the British media. 'Let's see what the British donors think about throwing these people on the scrap heap,' I wrote. APDA's management stopped me sending the letter.

I wanted to go and read the riot act to Oxfam in Addis. I became so heated that my own people at APDA again refused to let me go. They said they'd go themselves and solve this problem the Afar way, by reasoned discussion. Unfortunately, all the talking in the world didn't change things.

This was my first hard lesson in the fickle ways of international NGOs. I looked upon our work as similar to that of being a parent. When your child turns sixteen, you don't tell him or her that time's up, and throw them out on the street. If you're a true parent, until their development stage is over you give them a bed to sleep in, the use of the house, a bit of an allowance. Even when they do leave, you continue to take an interest. You ask how they are and whether they're coping with their finances; you try as a parent to be supportive until you know they're an adult and able to live without help. Somehow, the NGOs don't have to do that. They can, and do, cut off whole communities in mid-stream.

Community Aid Abroad (CAA) was a strong supporter of ours until a few years ago, when they suddenly decided they were no longer going to work in the Horn of Africa. They were leaving 'for strategic reasons', to concentrate on other areas. It's fine to concentrate on other areas, but why not leave what you've set up still operating? It's all very well to tell an individual that his work is finished, but there's a community out there expecting that person to do health or education work. After CAA bailed out, APDA took on 60 workers who would otherwise have been lost. We had to go into deficit to do it but the alternative was to abandon their programs.

There are fashions in international aid. At the moment HIV/AIDS is all the rage. Recently, one NGO suddenly called a halt right in the middle of one of our projects. They'd decided they were no longer going to do primary health work. From now on, AIDS was the thing. We were supposed to drop everything and start talking about condoms.

This isn't much help to people who've got malaria, anaemia, childbirth problems, and so on. Anyway, we never talk just about sexual health, we talk about whole body health. I told this NGO that it wouldn't work, but they insisted that from now on we concentrate only on AIDS. They said that if they caught us using their grant money for something else, we'd be out.

I broke the news to the clan leader in the area where the program had been operating. 'We're going to stop everything except discussions on sexual health.'

The old man said, 'What? You brought me what sort of talking today?'

'I told you, only sexual health from now on.'

'I can't believe this is coming from your mouth. We've just finished talking about all these people who have malaria and you want to talk about AIDS. We know how to control it, we've had a big talk about that one, but what about other things?'

'We can't do it.'

'Well, I'm coming with you to your office. I want to talk to your administration, because I can't believe this.'

'Come, please, but you'll see that it's not just me.'

He did come. We had a meeting and decided that APDA would somehow have to carry the burden.

You don't get development if you attach strings. I go back to my parent/child analogy. A child has a personality of their own. I might be the mother and want them to grow exactly to my framework with my ideals but, sorry, I can't do that, because inside that little person is an individual mind. Sure, if I gave birth to them, the child is a little bit like me and a little bit like the father, but they're a separate individual, and I've got to free that little individual and let them become the person they want to be. With Aisha, I must give her space. She's a new person, not exactly like Ismael or me and she's got to develop her personality. I can't pull her back and make her totally accountable to me.

It's the same with the developing world. The first world can't hold the third world accountable. This leads nowhere. What we're doing now is putting the whole thing in reverse gear. Despite all the funds that have gone into the country, we have more poverty in Ethiopia today than in the time of Haile Selassie. Most of those funds have been given on the paternalistic basis of holding the strings and not allowing the Ethiopians to use their own resources for their own ends.

Poverty isn't only lack of food and money, it's total disempowerment. It shouldn't be described only in economic terms, it should be defined by the fact that people are not permitted to run their own lives. We should trust each other enough to declare, 'In trust take this assistance.' This is the godly system, I think.

I know that there are instances of aid being misappropriated, but that's probably because it's been given in a way which has *encouraged* corruption. Maybe I'm too idealistic but, having lived with third-world people, I believe aid should be given at the basic level, and given so that those people can make their own decisions about how it's spent. Then they'll take responsibility and they'll do something very grand and very fine.

We've got 561 people doing hands-on work in their own communities. They are deciding the priorities – what's really damaging people's health, what's threatening their culture. In some places people are doing their own little campaigns. That's perfectly fine by us because then they're accountable for what they do.

It may seem a utopian ideal, but I think the big NGOs need to rethink the way they operate. The top-down model should be abandoned. Not using the knowledge of the local people should be abandoned. For example, there are aid workers in our region who are speaking a different language from Afar. How can they expect to be effective? Another language and culture have first of all to be appreciated for what they are. You can't go in with someone else's agenda and expect success.

*

It's my dream one day to be self-sufficient and no longer beholden to the international NGOs. Some Afar who live overseas assist us. A group called Afar Friends in Sweden has helped enormously. We also get help from Afar in Yemen, Sudan, Djibouti and Australia. New Zealand Afar are trying to get organised and it looks as though Canadian Afar might help us out a bit with education. Some Afar in America once helped us build a water source. So, they do try. It's probably up to me to try to motivate them more. It will involve travelling to those places. The difficult part will be finding the time.

We've tried to set up our own businesses to earn funds, with varied success. We got involved with salt mining in the Danakil Depression but we lost money. One clan leader gave us some land on the Awash River for farming. In the first year, we just covered our costs. This year we've made a tiny profit. The clan leader has said that if we need more land, he'll give it to us. Some Afar women are making bead jewellery and purses, which we're about to try to market, and there are other schemes being considered.

Ismael is always coming up with new ideas. He had a dream of opening a business bottling water. He said Logia water was perfect. He never did it and now lots of other factories have opened around Ethiopia, so the market's saturated. He wants to do more cross-border marketing of animals; he wants to set up a scheme so the Afar get better access to transport; he'd like to set up a chain of shops that run into the rural areas. He's got so many dreams that they just go on and on. He's Mr Positive – he runs on a dream. The funny thing is, my father was like that, he was Mr Positive too. They say that women marry the image of their father. Is that true? Ismael and I aren't experts at business or marketing, but we'll have to try something if we're ever to be self-sufficient.

Meanwhile, we're dependent upon the aid agencies and the government for our survival. During the famine of 2002/3 I was in the field vaccinating when I got an order from the government to come to the regional capital, Samara, for a meeting. I sent back a message that I couldn't because I was in the middle of a program. The word came back: 'This is a government order; you are coming in.'

Damn them, I thought. I had to put down the ice boxes, dismantle what I was doing and walk back to where our vehicles were. It was a horrible forced march for me and my team through a pitch-black night, unable to see where we were putting our feet, but I didn't want to waste time. I wanted to start work again as soon as possible.

It turned out that the world head of UNICEF was in the Afar region being taken around the drought areas. I was there basically to stand in the protocol line and shake her hand. Although she was supposed to be seeing the drought, World Vision had chosen to show her their area, which was essentially the last green area in Afar at the time.

The international media who were covering her visit were disappointed with the pictures they were getting. Some of the English-speaking journalists asked me where the real drought was. They were short of time and had to get their pictures back.

'I can show you the drought,' I said. 'Jump in the car, let's go.'

'Is it close by?'

'Not exactly. It'll take a while.'

'We can't leave this woman, we're reporting on her visit, we've got to follow her.'

In the end, someone started photographing a very crispy cow. All the crews focused on this dried-out husk of an animal. The UNICEF woman didn't see the dry places, people suffering from extreme thirst, the malnourished children. She saw a well-to-do area where World Vision had dug a well, and a dead cow. It was a fiasco – all so that World Vision could promote itself. It made me angry.

When the UNICEF boss returned to Addis, she held a news conference at the Sheraton Hotel, where she pledged that she would help the Afar region by any means she could. I never saw one single cent. It was all empty noise, as far as I can see.

Now that I've gone this far, I might as well ruffle a few more feathers and talk about the Church. Christ associated with prostitutes and thieves and lepers. He was right in the midst of those people showing them the love of God. So, the Church has got Christ to follow. If the Church doesn't stand for the people who haven't got justice, then what is the Church? If the Church is just running around cooking cakes and eating cucumber sandwiches, then I don't know what it's there for. We can all be nice and smiley and chatty-chat-chat but, at the end of the day, if we are an island surrounded by a sea of poverty and suffering and we shut our eyes, then we should shut the Church.

God made the world without poverty, in balance, so there doesn't have to be poor and rich. There's enough food in the world for everyone, but some people have taken twice what they need.

I was sitting next to an American man at a meeting recently. He remarked that North America was eating 80 per cent of the world's food. 'What do you think about that?' he asked.

Well, what can I think about it? I come from Ethiopia. Ethiopia doesn't have a say. It's pathetic me saying anything. It's about time *he* said something, because if he's not 80 per cent of the world's population yet he's eating 80 per cent of the world's food, what are the rest of the people getting? It's just utter greed.

The most revolting human trait is to sit in the corner and stuff yourself full without sharing. It's vulgar. It's inhuman. And that's what the Church should be fighting against.

Recently, someone from a big international NGO based in Addis telephoned Ismãel and said he wanted to bring some colleagues to Logia for a meeting. 'I'm expecting a good lunch from you,' he added.

We have a Yemeni cook who prepares food whenever we have a lot of people in town for meetings or new intakes of students. He usually cooks pretty basic stuff but, if asked to, he can produce a spread that you'd be proud to serve in a fine restaurant.

When Ismael told me what the fellow had demanded – and, make no mistake, it was a demand – I said, 'Just take it as a joke, let it slide.'

'No, we can't do that. I'll have to tell Hamid to start cooking. It's a business expense.'

Three well-fed-looking Ethiopian men turned up in a nice new Toyota Land Cruiser. They spent an hour or so talking with Ismael about a water purification program that they were funding. Then they, plus their driver, who looked pretty well-fed too, sat down to a magnificent spread. Hamid had outdone himself. He'd slaughtered two kids; there was goat cooked three different ways: stewed, roasted and fried. There was *injera*, two kinds of freshly baked bread, lentils, *shiro*, yellow rice, pasta, three different salads and, to finish, fruit, banana-and-coconut tart and coffee.

Ismael is an accomplished host. He made them laugh and feel at ease. I, on the other hand, was so annoyed that I wouldn't take part in the meeting, saying I had urgent work to attend to. I refused to join them for lunch either. At one stage I wandered over to where they were all stuffing themselves and commented, 'You people get so little to eat, you must be starving.'

I said it with a smile. The leader gave an uncomfortable little giggle and asked why I wasn't joining them. I told him I had work to do. It was all very polite and jolly but they got my message.

Ismael is probably right. You do have to flatter people and make them feel important, but the whole business just makes me mad. I couldn't let what happened that day pass without saying something.

I know I've got a big mouth sometimes. And there's a purely Australian larrikin streak in me which I can't keep down. Once we drove back to Addis from Logia with an American aid worker who'd been staying with us. We were in one of our beat-up utility trucks, and in the back was a pair of goats we were taking to an Afar man as a thank-you gift for some help he'd given us.

The American was booked in to the Sheraton, Addis Ababa's most prestigious hotel. It's a bizarrely opulent complex with a sweeping driveway, beautiful grounds and hot-and-cold-running flunkeys everywhere.

We rattled up the driveway in our disreputable vehicle and pulled up at the front entrance. A few guests in business suits stood about waiting for their rides. Bellboys hovered. A commissionaire wearing a red uniform and a bowler hat stepped forward to open the passenger door. He had to give it a good wrench, as it was stuck due to a minor accident, and it opened with a loud grinding noise. I got out and asked him if there were any spare rooms available.

'Of course, madam.'

'Good, I've got two goats here and they'd like one each.'

The commissionaire stared at me quizzically. I was wearing Afar clothing and was covered in dust from the journey. The guests observed the scene with interest. 'They can share, if that's not possible,' I added. 'They're good friends.'

After a long pause while he thought about it, the commissionaire allowed himself a small smile. You've got to have a laugh sometimes. If I didn't, I wouldn't survive.

CHAPTER 21

Because the Afar are an oral society, they are a very dramatic people. When they get excited, they shout and wave their arms about a lot. In conversation they'll sometimes illustrate a point with a proverb. It's their way of letting the information sink into the brain, and it works very well.

APDA has its own drama group which travels around from community to community putting on shows about things such as AIDS, FGM, health and hygiene, and so on. These little plays are full of fun and jokes, but they bring home a serious message. Recently there was an outbreak of acute watery diarrhoea in the Awra district. I've been referring to 'acute watery diarrhoea' all this time because that's the term the government insists upon. They haven't accepted that Ethiopia has cholera. We'd had a team of health workers down there for two months without a break, treating hundreds of people in very inaccessible country.

With this disease the first priority is to rehydrate the patient. You can treat them with Doxycycline, but we're reluctant to use it too much for fear that the people will develop resistance. If the disease reaches the resistant stage, then we'll be lost – thousands will die.

The answer to this problem, as it is for most health problems, is prevention. The people need clean water, they need good sanitation and hygiene. I remember once we were discussing a new water source in one settlement. The Imam said it would be a good idea because the people could then wash their clothes to wear to the mosque. I said, 'You can wash the clothes, but what about the body that goes inside? Why not wash the body?'

'You're talking too much like a town girl,' he said.

I said, 'I'm not town. This is not town culture or rural culture, it's health culture. If you don't want health culture, then we have to ask why not? Do you want sickness? Is that what you want?'

People are beginning to make the connection between cleanliness and health, but the big problem is the lack of water. Women have to bring it a long distance to the *deboita*, and it's a heavy load to carry. When they get it home, the first priority is thirst, not washing. So, people don't wash too often.

In some parts of Afar, such as Dallol, in the Danakil Depression, the situation is shocking. It's so dry that even when they pray, they ritually wash their face and hands with dust, not water. When it rains it's torrential. The desert looks like an ocean for a couple of hours, then it's all sucked into the ground.

We've given away hundreds of digging tools to dig ponds where the water will sit, so people can use it for washing. We're constructing underground concrete-rendered cisterns to collect rainwater, building dams and *boynas*. *Boynas* are an ingenious system used by the Afar for centuries to trap condensation from hot underground streams passing through volcanic land. The steam rises to the surface and makes wet patches. Afar find these wet patches and dig for what they call 'the eyes of the steam'. Above the eye, they build a closed-in rock house and you can hear the water dripping as it condenses. It works better at the colder time of year when they can collect up to 20 litres a day. It's perfectly clean water, and so hot you can dip your tea bag in and make a cup of tea. We've improved the *boynas* by rendering the rock with cement.

In fixed settlements we can build communal latrines and we've begun making our own soap to distribute to the communities. This is where the drama group comes in. They've written a play all about acute watery diarrhoea. In an entertaining way, it gets across the need to wash your hands, to boil water that may not be clean before drinking and all of those basic things which people in the west learn from childhood.

When I teach I do a lot of acting – some would say overacting. With health workers, I'm trying to get across some difficult concepts. As I mentioned before, to the Afar, blood is something like magic. There's good blood and bad blood. I've done everything but stand on my head to explain such concepts as the blood carrying oxygen and carbon dioxide, how it looks when it's got more oxygen and so on.

With traditional birth attendants I use a dummy mother and child, fifteen of which were donated by some health professionals in Adelaide. The dummy is a representation of a female pelvis containing a life-size black baby with placenta attached. I demonstrate how to deal with abnormal positioning, how the baby's born, by playing the midwife's part. I give lots of encouragement to the 'mother' and plenty of 'wah wah wahs' when the infant is born. The TBAs laugh at these antics but it's a great way to teach.

Our drama group performs plays and songs about *chat*, which is becoming a blight on not just Afar but all of Ethiopian society. *Chat* is a tree which is grown in the highlands. The leaves contain cathinone, an amphetamine-like stimulant. When people chew them, this induces mild euphoria and a feeling of well-being. As with speed, the heart beats faster, you drink lots of water and you don't sleep or eat. You lose your inhibitions. While a person is chewing *chat*, they're aroused, talkative, wide awake. When the effects wear off, they feel tired; they can be depressed or even suicidal. People who use *chat* tend to sit around neglecting work and their families, not to mention spending precious money on the stuff. If you get addicted, you can easily spend 20 or 30 birr per day, which is far more than the average Afar household has to live on. The men have to come to town to get *chat* and we are concerned that, under its influence, they'll go to commercial sex workers. There's then a high risk of them contracting venereal disease or AIDS.

Since the coffee price collapsed, many coffee growers have torn out their plants and replaced them with *chat*. You see bunches on sale everywhere. In the towns, it's quite common to see men lazing away the hours in the coffee shops, their mouths green with chewed leaf. It's already making big inroads into the pastoral society.

In Addis Ababa I spoke to a psychiatrist in Ethiopia's only psychiatric hospital. He said that 70 per cent of their cases were because of *chat*. Some of the patients had had severe mental illness. They'd given up washing and wandered the streets all day talking nonsense to themselves.

We've produced a poster which depicts a man sitting with his *chat* laid out and his *shisha*, or smoking device, beside him. His thought bubble shows him dreaming of skyscrapers – something outside Afar reality. His wife is looking at him with soulful eyes, thinking of food. Their baby's thought bubble shows a tin of Nido milk powder. Written across the top in Afar is the slogan, 'Everybody has his own thoughts.'

Another of APDA's campaigns is combating the practice of charcoal production. As you drive through the Afar region, you see beside the roads cylinder-shaped woven grass bags containing charcoal for sale. It's used as fuel for cooking. The local people make the charcoal by chopping down trees, which are needed for grazing. In a place where plants struggle to survive, it's madness to destroy the environment in this way.

Our environmental campaign is directed by Ahmed Ghidar, an Afar from Eritrea. Recently, Ahmed, Ismael and I went to Darsa Gita, where a meeting of clan leaders had been called to discuss the charcoal problem.

Darsa Gita is a small town of about 500 people in the middle of the Afar Regional State. As usually happens, we were looked after by the local people, who gave us a nice soft patch of dirt outside one of their dwellings to sleep on. As with all towns of this size, there's not one toilet in the entire place, so you have to walk to the edge of the settlement and find a quiet spot. The landscape being flat in all directions, it's more private if you can wait until dark. Water was scarce, so there was no question of having an all-over wash.

The elders held a meeting in one of the classrooms of the local school. About 40 turned up. They left their staffs and Kalash-nikovs stacked beside the door before going inside. Inside, there were rows of serious, weathered faces, the elders sitting at the desks like so many ancient schoolboys. There was the familiar aroma of warm bodies and smoke. You notice it in any confined space you are in with them, as their skin becomes impregnated from sitting around the fire inside the *deboita*. It's not an unpleasant smell at all, and far preferable to the sour body odour you sometimes encounter in the west.

One speaker after another rose to his feet to share his thoughts about the charcoal burning. Ahmed made a speech in which he told them that everyone should protect trees the same as they'd protect their eyes – for their children's sake. If they didn't, he said, there'd soon be no grazing land and they'd have to move further and further away.

As always, the elders showed particular respect when Ismael

spoke. He'd be embarrassed by me saying this, but he is an Afar hero and he's much loved because of his lifetime of work on behalf of his people.

After many hours, it transpired that the charcoal production was not just a piecemeal enterprise carried out by a few people to earn extra money, but an organised business controlled by three or four entrepreneurs. The meeting decided to call in these men to explain themselves.

Next day they reconvened. The entrepreneurs were told that there would be no more charcoal burning around Darsa Gita. Offenders would be required to face a *mablo*. If found guilty, they would be subject to fines ranging from two standing (live) goats, up to one standing cow, depending on the size and amount of trees destroyed.

This was a historic decision – hopefully, a model for similar outcomes in other areas. Government law had not been involved. It was Afar solving an Afar problem in the Afar way.

To reach the Afar, I've learned to think like an Afar. Teaching about sexually transmitted diseases such as HIV/AIDS is an example. Coming straight out with a lecture about condoms doesn't go down well in an Islamic society. You can get to the point by asking the question, 'Do we leave you in the hands of *Shaytan* [Satan], or do we help you? If *Shaytan* is telling you to do something that you shouldn't, then use a condom, they're easy to get.'

There will come a time when we'll no longer have to run these campaigns – when every Afar boy and girl will be educated. There are those who believe we shouldn't be bothering to educate pastoralists at all, that it would be better to leave their culture untouched. I believe that it's *only* through education that we'll save their way of life. Right now the Afar are hovering on the verge of cultural extinction. They're an anachronism in a fast-moving capitalist world whose driving motivation is the pursuit of wealth. The Ethiopian government, while making an effort to include Afar in their planning, has no real vision for pastoralists. They only understand villages and towns.

Education equals empowerment. An educated Afar can do exactly what he likes with his life. He can go and bang on the president's door if he feels like it. He can lobby the government. He can run his life instead of foreigners running it for him. He and his children can manage their own affairs. His children don't have to do what their father did; they can be doctors or business people or engineers if they want to.

I don't believe that everyone who receives an education will want to leave the pastoral life and settle in towns. I've got a friend who's living in Obno on the shores of Lake Abe on the Ethiopian side of the Djibouti border. He's a brilliant lawyer. He was born in Obno, went to school in Djibouti, and got a scholarship to study in France. He came first in his class at law school and went on to become a partner in a big law firm. After a few years he got fed up with western life and values and came back to Djibouti. He saw that the Afar had no place politically in Djibouti and decided to go back to where he was born.

He could have qualified for many positions in the European community. Instead, he's a camel herder. He's turned his back on the fancy French food and rich lifestyle, and he lives on camel's milk, with his clan, where his heart is at peace.

Our manager, Amin, lived in Canada for thirteen years with his wife and children, but couldn't put up with the shallow consumerism and loose morals of the west. He's been working with APDA for three years. He doesn't have the material possessions and comforts that he had over there but he would never exchange this life for the old one.

We had a young goat herder, Mohammad Hassan, who was selected by his community to study to be a health worker. When he first came to us and we put him in the class, he tried to squat on the table. He didn't know anything about chairs. His introduction to learning was a daunting experience. After the first few days, he came to me and confessed, 'I really want to learn but I didn't know you had to read and write. I don't think I can do it.'

I said, 'You'll have to, my son.'

He got himself a torch and spent his nights studying, long after everyone else had gone to sleep. He pushed himself hard and, out of a hundred students, he came eighth.

Mohammad's very clever, and very accurate with diagnoses. I want him to learn English now, and train as a nurse. He's had no formal education, though, so the government's not going to accept him for further education. They say he needs to have finished Year Twelve, which means he has no chance. But I'm sure he can do it. I've spoken to the head of the university in Tigray, who has said he's willing to experiment with cases like Mohammad's. First, we'll have to teach him English because the courses are in that language.

I believe Mohammad can be successful because he's very highly committed and he has a strong vision for his people. With education he could make huge changes. As a qualified nurse he could be in charge of a large area of primary health.

Abdu Youssef is a young man who was educated in Eritrea and Djibouti. Now and again in life you come across someone who's a real gem, and he's one of them. Abdu's a fast learner with great initiative. I want him to get training in development management, but there's nowhere in Ethiopia teaching such a course. There's a university in India called the Barefoot University, which is for students from developing countries. He could go there, perhaps, or he could probably even cope with a university in a first-world country, because his English is good and he has a very strong drive to learn. Abdu has a great passion for the Afar. He could be a leader in this organisation in the future.

The Afar shouldn't be dependent on outsiders as they are at the moment. We need our young people to be advocates – to write in magazines, speak strongly on the radio, to take up positions as nurses and doctors and lawyers and administrators. The improvement must come from them. They'll need to be mentally grounded and not allow themselves to be seduced by the west. My lawyer friend in Obno was able to make the right decisions, although to the west they would seem like the wrong decisions. No one in their right mind throws away a big income and all the comforts of middle-class life in France to go to live in the desert with a bunch of camels. But for him, that was totally the right thing to do.

Everyone requires balance. I've got two or three boys who I know will serve the Afar until the day they die, but they need to study in the west, get their qualifications and then come back to where they truly belong.

CHAPTER 22

When Ismael and I first married, I told him about my dysplasia and the doctor's warning of a one-in-three chance that our children could inherit the disease. We both thought it was a risk worth taking. Unfortunately, the odds were against us. Aisha has dysplasia.

I'd been looking for the signs ever since she was born and, sure enough, when she was a toddler, telltale nodules started to appear in her bones. It didn't affect her until much later, when she developed a pronounced deformity of the right arm. The ulna was very short, the radius was long and the cap of the radius shot out 3 centimetres beyond her elbow. By the time she reached her teens, her hand was turned in and writing had become a problem.

My brother David had a friend in Bowral who was an orthopaedic surgeon. He offered to perform a corrective operation. He took out the spur and put a plate in Aisha's upper arm to make it straight. Her arm is now cosmetically much better. She's still very conscious of it and wears long sleeves to cover up, but she's much happier and can now write without any pain. There won't be any need for further operations.

We took the opportunity while we were in Australia to visit each of my brothers and sisters in turn. They're scattered all over New South Wales, so Aisha got a chance to see something of country Australia. One day at Rosemary's place in Wyong on the New South Wales Central Coast, we ran out of bread. I volunteered to go to the supermarket and buy some. I hadn't asked what sort of bread she wanted. I didn't think I needed to, as, where I come from, bread is simply bread.

Not in Australia. Aisha and I were stunned at the choice on offer. There was bread with nuts on, bread with seeds on – or off; bread made out of this or that sort of flour; bread with oats in it, or pumpkin seeds, or honey, or . . . it was bewildering.

In Addis Ababa or Logia, we go to the bakery, tell them how many pieces we want and that's it. It's the same with milk. In Australia, milk is calcium-enriched – or not; light; skim; full cream with this or that added; long-life or fresh . . . it goes on and on.

I'm glad we don't have that choice. In my opinion, the west has gone overboard on choice. People say it's their right to consume. It's their right to have everything packaged and padded, see-through or not see-through, to own not one but two or three gas-guzzling motor cars which consume limited petroleum resources and contribute to the destruction of the planet. It's their right in Australia to own 15 million mobile phones, each one full of chips and plastic, so that they can make millions of unnecessary calls, and play games on them or take photographs. It's their right to chase obsessively after greater and greater wealth, more possessions, and consume more and more products while the rest of the world starves.

By contrast, it's against Afar culture to have individual wealth. You never see a rich Afar. And yet, you don't have anything like the rates of suicide and mental illness of the developed world. It seems to me that, for all their material wealth, people in the west are more and more lonely and out of contact with humanity; yet they regard the third world as primitives.

The west does not doubt that its life model is the best one. Along with the market economy, the west is very keen to impose democracy on the rest of us. Democracy is a western concept built on ideas that don't exist in Africa. I'm not at all sure that we need it. Why should we cast aside the traditional system of administration and respect which holds society together? If we didn't have outside ideas forced upon us, I'm sure the Afar would get along just fine.

It's amazing, isn't it, what thoughts a visit to the supermarket can lead to? But I should return to our visit to Australia.

I loved seeing my sisters and brothers again, and Aisha enjoyed meeting the aunts and uncles to whom she'd been writing for years. She missed her father terribly, though. And, for me, the visit was another reminder of the differences between myself and the rest of the family. I admire my sisters and I love them dearly, but I couldn't live like them. If for some reason I had to go back to Australia permanently, I'm not sure that I could cope. Every time I return, it's a shock. I'm amazed at the technology, the pace of life and the rampant consumerism. Although none of my sisters is particularly rich, they live in absolute luxury compared with me – yet I wouldn't change my life for theirs.

Ismael feels the same way. It surprises many people that, having married an Australian woman, he'd rather live in Ethiopia than in the west. During our first trip to Australia he was on a tram in Melbourne. The conductor was an Ethiopian. While they were chatting he asked Ismael what he was doing in the country. When he heard that he was just visiting, the conductor volunteered to help him get residency. He apparently knew all the angles. He could hardly believe it when Ismael told him he wasn't interested.

*

A couple of months after we returned home from that last trip, there was a massive outbreak of 'acute watery diarrhoea' in southern Afar. In the days that followed, I saw human suffering on a scale that I had not seen for a long time.

I was working with three government health workers. For ten days and nights, we worked practically around the clock, snatching a few hours' sleep only when we were absolutely exhausted. On the first day we saw 70 patients; on the second day, 90; and more than 50 per day after that. Every one of them needed immediate rehydration to stop them dying from extreme vomiting and diarrhoea. We considered ourselves lucky to lose only five people during the ten days. Of these five, three were very young children.

The children were the most difficult to treat. Often we could not locate their tiny veins to insert an IV tube. One baby was so far gone when she arrived that she collapsed and died within minutes, before we could begin treatment.

The outcome with another little girl, however, was a miracle. We had spent a long time – too long – working on her, trying and trying to put an IV into her veins and failing. I then put a naso-gastric tube in and started slowly giving her oral rehydration solution, ORS – a sugar and salt mix in sachets made up by UNICEF. Still she continued to vomit. She was very dehydrated, with deep sunken eyes, and was completely inactive. Her elderly grandmother was her 'mother' because her real mother was at home in the last stage of pregnancy.

The old woman was exhausted, having held the desperately ill child for over 24 hours. Her clothes were soaked in vomit and diarrhoea. She was ancient, with deep lines etched into a weather-beaten face. She'd seen a lot of life – and death. She said her granddaughter's breathing pattern was typical of a child who was about to die, and she was resigned to the fact that she was going to lose her. I thought that she was very probably right, but still I told her that we would not give up. I told her to go and wash her clothes while I stayed and nursed the child.

This, she did. When she came back I left her in order to attend to other patients, but kept popping back until late at night. We continued to drip the rehydration mix slowly into the girl. At about one in the morning I decided to lie down for a while and rest but before I did I checked on her again. She seemed slowly to be coming round. I turned the drip off, not wanting to overload. I mixed a litre of ORS in an empty water bottle and left it by the old woman, telling her to give the girl sips now and then.

At three a.m., I got up to see her and the other patients who needed regular checking. I found the old woman sound asleep. The toddler had got herself out from under her blanket, located the bottle and was trying to balance it so that she could take a sip herself. It was so exhilarating to see her that I picked her up and kissed her. In the morning she was bright and happy and playing with her grandma!

CHAPTER 23

There's a constantly shifting population at our compound in Logia. People turn up, stay a while then move on. They're Afar who are down on their luck, sometimes women escaping a bad marriage, young men who need assistance with higher education, members of Ismael's clan who might need a bit of help. There are a few who are pretty much permanent residents. One is Fatuma Aboobakar, a woman who I'd guess is about 30. Like most she doesn't know her exact age. Fourteen years ago Fatuma suffered terrible injuries during childbirth. This is a common plight all over Ethiopia. No matter where they live, even in the western world, 10 per cent of all women will have some kind of complication while giving birth. If they live in a place like Australia, they simply go to hospital and have a Caesarean or a forceps delivery. In the Ethiopian highlands or deep in the Afar desert, they may be a couple of days' walk from the nearest road, let alone a hospital. A woman with obstructed labour squats in the *deboita*, enduring the agony sometimes for five or six days. By the time the baby is born it is dead and the mother may be left with a hole, or fistula, in her bladder and sometimes also in her rectum. Her bodily wastes constantly drain out through her vagina. Because she is so offensive to be near, her husband invariably divorces her and she is shunned by the rest of the community. These women live lives of utter misery.

The lucky ones may hear about a hospital in Addis Ababa run by a wonderful Australian obstetrician, Dr Catherine Hamlin. Catherine and her husband, Reg, came to Ethiopia in 1959 and made it their life's work to help the fistula sufferers. In 1975 they built a hospital dedicated solely to fistula surgery. Since it opened, they've performed over 30,000 operations and do so completely free of charge. In all but the most severe cases, the women are cured and life begins again. We send quite a few women to Addis to the Fistula Hospital. Fatuma spent two years there but her injuries were so severe that they couldn't completely cure her. To give her some semblance of a normal life, they performed an operation in which the ureters are brought out to the stomach wall and collect the urine in a bag.

Fatuma can't go back to a rural area because she needs to be meticulous about hygiene. Also, her kidneys are damaged, so the rural water isn't suitable. While she's been living with us we've given her a job and she's learned to read and write. She can't marry again, so she'll stay in Logia for the foreseeable future.

Until recently we had another Fatuma, Fatuma Yusef, who was also an ex-fistula patient who was only partially cured. Fatuma learned to read and write, and she absolutely loved it. She used to lie on her mat outside, reading until late at night. She's gone back to her home and we've given her a job as a women's extension worker. Fatuma is a smart woman. She'll go far.

One of the compound's favourites is Aisha. A slim little girl who, according to her mother, is twelve. She comes from the southern part of Afar. When she was a baby her parents divorced. Her mother remarried and the new husband didn't care about Aisha. When more children came along Aisha became the family drudge, herding the goats and being pretty much neglected. At the age of six or seven she contracted measles which badly affected her eyes. One eye is scarred so that the cornea and the conjunctiva are adhering to the lids. We found a very clever surgeon in Addis who's helping break the adhesions and putting in minute transplants from inside Aisha's mouth onto the rough areas to stop them re-adhering.

When Aisha came to us she was blind. Her eyes were full of pus, and she was anaemic and malnourished. Now she's regained the sight in one eye. We've had her for two years and she'll need more operations yet. Hopefully, we'll get her reunited with her mother one day. In the meantime, she's happy being here and looking forward to learning to read and write soon.

There are a couple of women with us at the moment who are HIV-positive. They're staying while they take AIDS medicine.

We have with us, too, several young Afar men in their late teens who are refugees from Eritrea. Many of them come here to evade the draft that would cause them to end up fighting in the interminable war against Ethiopia which is still going on sporadically at the border. No one wants to die for such a pointless cause. We let them stay at the compound, and feed them and see that they get an education. Some refugees have come from Eritrea after being incarcerated for the most spurious reasons. One young man spent two and a half years in an underground cell. He couldn't stand up or put his legs out straight. He was sitting with his knees bent and couldn't even turn from side to side, the walls were so close. He never saw light or heard a friendly voice. Three times a day, they gave him bread, and sometimes a thin soup of lentils with the bread; never anything else. His only exercise was being taken out before dawn and late at night to go to the toilet. I asked him how he didn't go mad. He said he wasn't very well educated, but he'd heard there was a man called Mr Nelson Mandela who'd been imprisoned for many years and that man kept his patience and eventually he got his freedom. This young man was considered to be an Ethiopian spy but he was just an innocent boy. He told me that many people didn't get out of that prison alive and many went mad.

The regime in Eritrea, still ruled by Afeworke, is paranoid about any opposition. Eritrean soldiers came 57 kilometres inside Ethiopia, kidnapped one of my health workers, Abdella, and three others, at a wedding ceremony, and took him back to Eritrea. I tried to get information about him from the Red Cross and the UN peacekeeping force but no one could find out anything.

Three years later he just appeared again. He'd been in an underground prison they've dug at a place about 30 kilometres inside the border. They'd accused him of being a spy, but that's absurd. His name was just on a list or something. When he came out, his coordinator said he couldn't keep Abdella on, as he was no longer normal. He wouldn't stay with his wife, he didn't seem to know himself, he wandered about everywhere and they couldn't rely on him.

Eventually, the clan elders sat him down and made him realise he had a wife and children, and that the past was the past and he had to leave it behind him.

As I write this, I have 52 health workers combating an outbreak of 'acute watery diarrhoea' down near the Awash River. We didn't have the money to pay for a treatment campaign, so I held a meeting and asked my colleagues what we should do. I said, 'Will we just listen to the reports of the deaths? Is that what we'll do?'

They said, 'No, we can't do that, Maalika. You'll have to send some people in.'

We pulled out all the budgets, and took a little bit of money from here and a little bit from there. We can't send health workers out on empty stomachs. They have to have food and they have to be paid; they have families and responsibilities like everyone else.

My other big concern right now is that the region is slipping into famine. The rains which usually come in June have not arrived in Afar. Famines here are not like those famines you see on TV. Afar hunger is different from highland hunger. Highland hunger, as I saw in Alamata when I first went to Ethiopia, and again in the 1984 famine, kills en masse. Afar die alone. They don't come to the roadside, or form into camps, they just quietly starve to death out in the desert without the world hearing anything about it. A group from Germany has just agreed to help by buying up lentils for pregnant women and breastfeeding mothers. I've got health workers and women's extension workers identifying needs and distributing supplies to these women. Now I'll buy up baby food and distribute it to babies who are too young to have teeth and can't swallow hard food. It's a hand-to-mouth way of dealing with a huge problem, but that's the way we have to work.

The Afar region is now graded as having the highest level of rural poverty per head of population in Ethiopia. This is not just an economic problem, it's a political problem. The government doesn't have their interests as a priority. I sometimes can't help thinking that, in their eyes, the Afar are expendable, and that's another battle we have to fight. It's a desperate fight, very exhausting and frustrating. I've been asked to go to two meetings in Addis Ababa in a couple of weeks, one in the Sheraton Hotel and one in the Hilton. It makes me vomit to go into those places to discuss issues about the Afar. It gives you an idea of where these bureaucrats are coming from. Why the hell are they having their meetings in the Sheraton and the Hilton to begin with? What are they going to do in those meetings? Are they going to change anything? I know they're not, but I have to attend because if I don't, I'll be asked why.

Recently, someone asked me why I didn't just let all these problems slide by once in a while. The need for justice is a very big thing with me. It's a bit like if you were living in a tall apartment in Sydney and could see into someone else's kitchen. In that apartment lives an old lady. She's a little bit blind, and a little bit slow and not good on her legs. You see that her gas stove is on and the kitchen curtains have caught alight. What are you going to do? Are you going to pull your blind down and imagine that it never happened? Are you going to yell out the window and say, 'Hey, granny, wake up, the kitchen's ablaze', or are you going to go and help her? You have to make a decision. You can make that decision about something very particular like this old lady, or about something as big as the future of a whole race. If we see, if we know, then we have to do something.

So many Europeans have asked me why I don't burn out. I don't know about this burnout. I think burnout is when you are the one who failed. You've finished, you've failed, you've made a mess. You took all the responsibility on your little shoulders and it didn't work out, so you can't continue. Well, I don't do that. I can be a cog in a wheel but I'm not the whole machine. There are plenty of other players, and if I go there'll be plenty coming behind. Nobody's indispensable. Everyone's obsessed with individual achievement in the west. Here, community is the thing – where are the Afar going? I mean, who gives a damn where I'm going, that's not important. The question is, where is the community going?

I don't think I will ever be an Afar. I don't feel anything for nationality, really. One of the problems I see in the world is this strange idea of 'I'm a Chinese, I'm an Australian, I'm a Mexican.' Having a passport is very nice but why do we have to look at each other as being different? I don't feel like an Australian. I don't know what nationality I am. I know that the Afar people relate to me with love, which is a tremendous privilege. They accept all my stupidity, all my foolishness. I have terrible temper tantrums, I'm not a very nice person, but they accept me because I go through everything with them.

Ismael and I have made no provision for the future. Superannuation? Saving for old age? Never heard of it. What's the point? Life's got to finish sometime. I think insurance is just a way to tie yourself down. You've got to face death, my friend. I never heard of anyone who escaped death. I know that if Ismael or I dies, the community will look after Rammid and Aisha. That's our insurance.

Ismael used to dream that he'd retire one day and run an ostrich farm. We'd sit around and be idle, and talk about the good old days. I have a fantasy from time to time that I'd like to have a little *deboita* somewhere with a few goats and live a simple life without any worries. Aisha hates the idea. 'How would I come to see you, Mummy?' she says.

I tell her, 'Well, my dear, you'll just have to.'

Like Ismael's ostrich farm, I know it'll never happen.

I think I'll probably just keep working until one day I drop. Then they can bury me under a pile of stones in the desert, the Afar way. And I'll be perfectly happy with that.

In the meantime, the Afar are poised at a critical point in their evolution. What happens in the next ten years or so will determine whether their unique and beautiful culture survives or is destroyed, as so many others have been destroyed. Just south of Logia, they're building a huge dam across the Awash River. The plan is to irrigate 60,000 hectares of land where they'll grow sugar. They say this will transform the region and give employment to 100,000 people. The Afar who live there now will be displaced, and you can bet that most of the jobs will go to imported highlanders. That's what usually happens with these development schemes.

The Afar urgently need better education and health. They need to learn about money and business. I know that, once learned, these are the very things that may entice them into the mainstream. The challenge for them will be to use those advantages to better their own culture. It would be tragic indeed if it were to die.

That is our task.

God knows, there's plenty left to do.

AFTERWORD

Six months after visiting Valerie in Logia, I returned to Ethiopia to work with her on the manuscript of this book. It was June – midsummer – a bad time to be in Afar country. I planned to stay with Valerie in Addis Ababa, where it would be cooler and we'd be away from the distractions of APDA's busy headquarters.

The flat which Valerie and Ismael rent is on the fourth floor of a building on the corner of two busy roads in Olympia. In a car park below, the well-to-do pull up in their Range Rovers and BMWs beside the Café Parisienne. Uniformed waiters help them park, then bring their cappuccinos right to the cars. For trendy Addisites, it's the latest thing. Half a block away there's an ugly yellow building housing expensive jewellery and clothing shops, airline offices, banks, travel agents. A hundred metres in the other direction are a couple more trendy cafés and a supermarket.

Olympia is Addis Ababa's version of a middle-class suburb, yet it bears no resemblance to its western equivalent. In between the cafés and fancy highrises are shabby little businesses struggling to survive. As I walk towards Valerie's apartment building, I step around a beggar woman and four small children, one just a baby, huddling under a thin blanket on the footpath. A young man with legs withered by polio balances on crutches, begging. A blind man taps along with one hand held out for alms. The paving erupts here and there with abandoned excavations. The air is acrid with exhaust smoke. Shoeshine boys ply their trade; women crouch over braziers grilling corn cobs; hawkers offer fake designer watches, cheap clothing, lottery tickets. Forget the cappuccinos; for these people each day is a fight for survival.

To reach Valerie's flat you walk up dimly lit stairs. There's no lift. There are cigarette butts on the steps and plastic bags of rubbish in the corners of the landings. The surfaces look as though they have not been cleaned since the place was built. For Addis Ababa, this is not a bad address. A few tenants have scribbled their names on the walls beside their doors. The occupant of the flat directly below Valerie is a professor.

Valerie's flat has two bedrooms, a kitchen, bathroom and tiny lounge room. APDA's office is one floor above. There's a secretary, a couple of administrative staff and Solomon, the driver, who runs messages around town. When I enter, Valerie is on the phone to Ismael in Logia. She looks even more careworn than I remember – with good cause, I soon learn. She has spent the last two weeks with a team of health workers fighting yet another outbreak of – what the hell, let's call it what it is – cholera. June is the beginning of the rainy season. Although it has been raining every day in Addis, the rains have not come to Afar. The region is slipping into famine, exacerbated by a locust plague which has decimated what little fodder remained. Many pastoralists have migrated to the Awash River and it is there that the disease has run rife among them.

A young man in his mid-twenties, climbing a tree to cut fodder, had lost his footing and fallen to the ground, injuring his spine. He was in severe pain with a shattered vertebra and one leg was paralysed. His family had taken him to a local government hospital, where he'd been x-rayed. They'd told him there was nothing they could do.

Valerie found him lying in his *deboita* in agony and brought him with her to Addis. There was no point taking him to the government hospital, the Black Lion. He could wait months before they'd admit him and he'd probably die in the meantime. So, the night before, they'd taken him to a private hospital. They'd brought his brother to wash and stand by him. When they pushed the trolley into a lift, his brother had panicked. 'He's disappeared,' he said, trembling with fright. Valerie calmed him down and took him up the stairs.

He'd been admitted, but the hospital was demanding the full amount of money for a neurosurgeon to operate before they would do anything. The boy's parents had managed to raise 1000 birr, about A\$170, with great difficulty. Valerie had pledged what little she had in her personal account, but they were still short. She was discussing with Ismael what to do.

For Ismael, the solution was simple. The young man needed an operation right away. They'd use their joint salary to make up the shortfall.

As I should have expected, the next few days were not exactly tranquil. As we worked, Valerie was constantly interrupted by calls demanding her attention. She had the injured boy to deal with – he would be relieved of his pain but one leg would remain permanently paralysed; she had to arrange to return two patients from the Fistula Hospital back to their homes in Afar; she had to attend meetings with NGOs and the government; she had to visit Aisha's school to discuss a poor report. None of this quelled her energy for a moment. As we worked, she would now and then break off to rail passionately against the rapacious private hospital system, the even worse public system, the inefficiency of big NGOs, the sluggishness of government, the apathy of the west. In the evenings after we'd finished for the day, she'd stay up late working on reports. As usual, there were a few Afar in residence – a couple of men sleeping on the lounges in the flat and a couple more on camp beds in the office.

We finished the manuscript at last. Next morning, as we sat over our breakfast of bread and *shiro*, Valerie was in a reflective mood. Maybe I know why. If things have gone well, there's a warm feeling when you finish writing a memoir. A bond has formed. Our work was done and soon our book, like a child leaving home, would have to make its way in the world. In tune with the mood, I asked a question I'd long been wondering. Did she miss female company?

'Yes', she said, 'that's the thing I miss most.'

For twenty years Valerie has not had an intimate conversation with a woman friend, in which she can talk about the things that matter to women. She knows many Afar women but that kind of relationship with an Afar would be impossible. 'I pine for it,' she said quietly. 'The closest I can get to it is with Aisha. She came from me and now she's my closest friend. A sixteen-year-old girl.'

Even then, there are things a mother cannot talk about with her daughter. Only a woman could fully understand the ache in Valerie's heart.

Rammid was staying in the flat, and little Aisha from Logia, who was down to see her eye doctor. Also, there was Medena, a seventeen-year-old girl whom Valerie and Ismael are educating. She lives in the flat with Aisha. Medena's mother died of AIDS three years ago. Her mother's sister had died and another sister just disappeared. They've been educating her since she was seven. Ismael feels obliged because the mother claimed Medena's father was Afar. They'll never really know but, as far as they're both concerned, it doesn't matter.

That day, Valerie had a rare few hours to spare between meetings. We all went to a fun parlour. It was on the third floor of a new upmarket shopping centre, a spacious room painted in bright primary colours, crammed with video games and karaoke machines. Lights flashed, the air was loud with the sounds of whistles, sirens, fake gunfire, racing cars, shrieking children. Excited hordes ran from one game to the next, watched fondly by their well-dressed parents. It was a garish slice of imported culture, which the kids adored.

This rare family treat would, of course, have been perfect if Ismael had been there too. In distant Logia, he had just received awful news. When we returned to the flat, he rang to say that one of APDA's health workers had died in the cholera epidemic. Mohammad Ali Boori was his name.

Valerie put down the receiver and stood in silence, looking off into some far interior space. No histrionics, no tears; at least, not then. I think what I was seeing was a moment or two – no more than that – of despair, before she steeled herself for the fight once more. Mohammad Ali was recently married and had a new baby. He and Valerie had been through hard times together, and they'd shared some triumphs, too. He was one of her most valued people. A few days earlier, she had been working beside him saving lives, and now suddenly he was gone. She is used to seeing death but this death was different. This was family. One of her own.

That very morning during those quiet moments of introspection, she had recited for me her favourite prayer.

> To give and not count the cost.
> To fight and not heed the wounds.
> To toil and not seek rest.
> To labour and not ask for any reward,
> save knowing that I do your will.

It seemed to me that, for all the words we had written, those few lines captured best the essence of Maalika. Next day we said our goodbyes and she made ready to return north, to the desert and her people.

John Little

Addresses for donations to APDA

Australia
Donations to APDA can be made via their Australian partners
AngliCORD.
PO Box 139
East Melbourne VIC 8002
Tel: (03) 9495 6100
www.anglicord.org.au

Barefoot Initiative
PO Box 318
Mt Barker SA 5251
Tel: 0401 801 881
www.barefootinitiative.org

Canada
APDA Canada
1220 Merivale Rd
App#408
Ottawa \Ontario L1Z-8P2
Tel: 613 266 0929
Email: harsile@sympatico.ca

Sweden
Afar Friends in Sweden
PO Box 25156
S-750 25
Uppsala
Email: afarsolidarity@yahoo.se

APDA's website
www.apdaethiopia.org